"The appearance in this se_ Karl Marx, both the man and his thought, is a timely that Marxism remains a vibrant ideological influence in the world. Unshackled from his twentieth-century exploiters and the stark disparities that misshaped popular imagination for most of that century, Marx's ideas are now receiving fresh, rejuvenating attention. In this brief introduction, Dennison usefully distinguishes Marx from Marxism, sketches Marx's turbulent biography, and then traces the contours of his ideas from the vantage point of his post-Hegelian materialistic philosophy of history. The philosophy-of-history approach is well conceived and effectively sets the stage for Dennison's distinct contribution: an extended presuppositional critique of Marx's naturalistic humanism, demonstrating that Cornelius Van Til's ideas are at least as vibrant as Marx's, and the gospel far more compelling."

—**Bruce P. Baugus**, Associate Professor of Philosophy and Theology, Reformed Theological Seminary, Jackson

"Marx remains a key figure in the politics, economics, and history of the past two centuries. Christians might see him as dangerous or insightful—or both—but in any case we ignore him to our own detriment. Bill Dennison presents both the man and his legacy in a way that introduces the basics and gives readers the tools to pursue a fuller view, including a Reformed perspective as a framework for understanding. Readers will benefit from Dennison's clarity and guidance."

—**Kevin R. den Dulk**, Paul B. Henry Chair in Political Science, Calvin College

"Christians wanting to know how to think about Karl Marx would do well to read this volume. Directly examining the texts of Marx, Dennison carefully guides his readers through the great thinker's philosophy of history. But this guidance is neither a superficial hatchet job nor a mindless embrace. Instead, scholars and neophytes alike will benefit from Dennison's strategy of critical appreciation: appreciation for Marx's real insights—such as his analysis of capitalism—but also a critique rooted in the revelation of God in history. What readers will find is an evaluation of Marx as an eschatological thinker done from the perspective of the eschatology revealed in Scripture."

—**Andrew Kaufmann**, Assistant Professor of Political Science, Northwest University

"There are few good, concise books on Karl Marx, his philosophy, and his worldview. There are still fewer written from a biblical, Reformed perspective. This solid treatment by Bill Dennison fills an important niche. I highly recommend it to anyone looking for a scholar whom they can trust to offer a terse summation of Marx and how Marx's ideas should be viewed in the light of a Christian Reformed worldview. Here we see Marx examined, at last, from the vantage of innocence, sin, grace, and God's plan versus Marx's plan. Alas, this should be how Marx is *always* viewed. But it has taken Bill Dennison to finally do the job. For that, we owe him a debt of gratitude."

—**Paul G. Kengor**, Professor of Political Science and Executive Director, Center for Vision & Values, Grove City College

"Karl Marx is a difficult and complex thinker, giving rise to numerous controversies and schools of thought about what he actually meant. In this fine book, William Dennison displays a command of both Marx's own writings and the various disputes among Marxist schools of thought. Dennison uses Marx's philosophy of history both as a useful entry point to his thought and as a locus for an illuminating contrast with a Reformed philosophy of events that proclaims God's providential activity in history."

—**Daniel Edward Young**, Professor of Political Science, Northwestern College

Praise for the Great Thinkers Series

"After a long eclipse, intellectual history is back. We are becoming aware, once again, that ideas have consequences. The importance of P&R Publishing's leadership in this trend cannot be overstated. The series Great Thinkers: Critical Studies of Minds That Shape Us is a tool that I wish I had possessed when I was in college and early in my ministry. The scholars examined in this well-chosen group have shaped our minds and habits more than we know. Though succinct, each volume is rich, and displays a balance between what Christians ought to value and what they ought to reject. This is one of the happiest publishing events in a long time."

—**William Edgar**, Professor of Apologetics, Westminster Theological Seminary

"When I was beginning my studies of theology and philosophy during the 1950s and '60s, I profited enormously from P&R's Modern Thinkers Series. Here were relatively short books on important philosophers and theologians such as Nietzsche, Dewey, Van Til, Barth, and Bultmann, by scholars of Reformed conviction such as Clark, Van Riessen, Ridderbos, Polman, and Zuidema. These books did not merely summarize the work of these thinkers; they were serious critical interactions. Today, P&R is resuming and updating the series, now called Great Thinkers. The new books, on people such as Aquinas, Hume, Nietzsche, Derrida, and Foucault, are written by scholars who are experts on these writers. As before, these books are short—around 100 pages. They set forth accurately the views of the thinkers under consideration, and they enter into constructive dialogue, governed by biblical and Reformed convictions. I look forward to the release of all the books being planned and to the good influence they will have on the next generation of philosophers and theologians."

Karl

MARX

GREAT THINKERS

A Series

Series Editor
Nathan D. Shannon

Karl
MARX

William D. Dennison

P&R PUBLISHING
P.O. BOX 817 • PHILLIPSBURG • NEW JERSEY 08865-0817

Scripture quotations are from the ESV® Bible (*The Holy Bible, English Standard Version*®), copyright © 2001 by Crossway, a publishing ministry of Good News Publishers. Used by permission. All rights reserved.

ISBN: 978-1-62995-150-8 (pbk)
ISBN: 978-1-62995-151-5 (ePub)
ISBN: 978-1-62995-152-2 (Mobi)

Printed in the United States of America

Library of Congress Cataloging-in-Publication Data

Names: Dennison, William D., 1949- author.
Title: Karl Marx / William D. Dennison.
Description: Phillipsburg : P&R Publishing, 2017. | Series: Great thinkers | Includes bibliographical references and index.
Identifiers: LCCN 2017028326| ISBN 9781629951508 (pbk.) | ISBN 9781629951515
  (epub) | ISBN 9781629951522 (mobi)
Subjects: LCSH: Marx, Karl, 1818-1883. | Philosophy, Marxist.
Classification: LCC B3305.M74 D466 2017 | DDC 335.4092 [B] --dc23
LC record available at https://lccn.loc.gov/2017028326

To Cale Horne
Former excellent student,
presently a tremendous colleague and friend

CONTENTS

SERIES INTRODUCTION

Amid the rise and fall of nations and civilizations, the influence of a few great minds has been profound. Some of these remain relatively obscure even as their thought shapes our world; others have become household names. As we engage our cultural and social contexts as ambassadors and witnesses for Christ, we must identify and test against the Word those thinkers who have so singularly formed the present age.

The Great Thinkers series is designed to meet the need for critically assessing the seminal thoughts of these thinkers. Great Thinkers hosts a colorful roster of authors analyzing primary source material against a background of historical contextual issues, and providing rich theological assessment and response from a Reformed perspective.

Each author was invited to meet a threefold goal, so that each Great Thinkers volume is, first, *academically informed*. The brevity of Great Thinkers volumes sets a premium on each author's command of the subject matter and on the secondary discussions that have shaped each thinker's influence. Our authors identify the most influential features of their thinkers' work and address them with precision and insight. Second, the series maintains a high standard of *biblical and theological faithfulness*. Each volume stands on an epistemic commitment to the "whole counsel of God" (Acts 20:27), and is thereby equipped for fruitful critical engagement. Finally, Great Thinkers texts are *accessible*, not burdened with jargon or unnecessarily difficult vocabulary. The goal is to inform and equip the reader as effectively as possible through clear writing, relevant analysis, and incisive, constructive critique. My hope is that this series will distinguish itself by striking with biblical faithfulness and the riches of Reformed tradition at the central nerves of culture, cultural history, and intellectual heritage.

Bryce Craig, president of P&R Publishing, deserves hearty thanks for his initiative and encouragement in setting the series in motion and seeing it through. Many thanks as well to P&R's director of academic development, John Hughes, who assumed, with cool efficiency, nearly every role on the production side of each volume. The Rev. Mark Moser carried much of the burden in the initial design of the series, acquisitions, and editing of the first several volumes. And the expert participation of Amanda Martin, P&R's editorial director, was essential at every turn. I have long admired P&R Publishing's commitment, steadfast now for over eighty-five years, to publishing excellent books promoting biblical understanding and cultural awareness, especially in the area of Christian apologetics. Sincere thanks to P&R, to these fine brothers and sisters, and to several others not mentioned here for the opportunity to serve as editor of the Great Thinkers series.

Nathan D. Shannon
Seoul, Korea

FOREWORD

As I was growing up in Britain in the decades before the fall of the Berlin Wall, Marxism loomed over my childhood like a very real possible future. Ignorant of the full extent of the economic disaster on which the Eastern Bloc was built, I pondered whether Communism might well carry the day and prove to be the meaning of history. Yet in 1989, all that changed. Mikhail Gorbachev's policies of glasnost and perestroika had unleashed social and cultural forces that the old guard was ultimately unable to contain or control, and first the various Soviet satellites and then the Soviet Union itself collapsed. For a while, it looked as though the end of history had truly come, that Western liberal capitalism had triumphed.

Of course, such a view looks hopelessly naive today. The rise of militant Islam and the resurgence of the old, powerful gods of nationalism and ethnic chauvinism have proved deadly foes to the West's pitifully little gods of consumerism and sexual hedonism. To quote conservative journalist Rod Dreher, you cannot fight something with nothing. And the West has found that its emphases on relativism and multiculturalism do indeed tend to amount to nothing in the ongoing struggles within the culture.

Amid all this flux, there has been a renewed interest in the life and thought of Karl Marx. In the last few years, two major scholarly biographies have appeared in English, both setting him carefully in his nineteenth-century context. His works continue to sell well in English. Marxist thinkers such as Terry Eagleton produce works that engage the various pathologies of the modern West from an avowedly Marxist perspective. Marx's popularity is clearly rising with a young, post-1989 generation for whom Marxism as a term does not summon up images of food shortages, gulags, and ghastly East German architecture, but rather the ideals of freedom, equality, and social justice.

Furthermore, if Marxism seemed in its death throes in 1989, today it is arguable that, to use Michael Hanby's arresting phrase, "Marx has won" in the sense that everything is now political. The later Marx of *Capital* may now be obsolete, but the Marx of the early manuscripts, the Marx who offered the foundation of a comprehensive view of reality and history in political terms, sets the terms of debate on campuses and in the media, for whom everything has to be seen in terms of political power and political struggle.

For these reasons, knowledge of Marx's life and thought is vital for any Christian who wants to understand why the Western world of today thinks the way it does. Marx is one of those elite philosophers, along with Plato, Montaigne, Rousseau, Nietzsche, Freud, Sartre, and Camus, who have a distinct literary bent. This makes him delightful to read, especially in works such as *The Communist Manifesto* and *The German Ideology*. But as with these other thinkers, his limpid prose can hide the fact that his thought is still subtle and requires both contextualization and some pointers for interpretation. Also, his vast literary output is daunting. The new reader needs guidance on how to tackle such a vast array of written work.

That is why it is a pleasure to recommend this little guide by Bill Dennison. Bill and I may not agree on every aspect of interpretation and critique of Marx, but this volume is a helpful and reliable entry point into his thought. Offering both clear exposition and trenchant Christian critique, Bill makes Marx accessible to the neophyte. This is a short, yet informative book on an important thinker whose specter continues to haunt the West. Read it, then read Marx, and think on these things.

Carl R. Trueman
William E. Simon Visiting Fellow in Religion and Public Life
Princeton University;
Paul Woolley Professor of Church History
Westminster Theological Seminary

PREFACE

During my doctoral studies at Michigan State University in the mid-1980s, I seriously considered doing my dissertation on Karl Marx after studying his thought under the direction of my philosophy advisor, Richard Peterson, an expert in nineteenth-century social and political philosophy. As I engaged the journey of Marx's family from Judaism to Protestant Christianity, I became fascinated with drawing parallels between Lutheran theology and his secular analysis of social and political thought. Although Professor Peterson was genuinely intrigued with the subject, he convinced me not to pursue this task since at that time there were a vast number of dissertations being written on Marx. In such an environment, he thought it would be extremely difficult to distinguish my work from others, so he encouraged me to continue with my original plan to work on Rudolf Bultmann—which I did.

There remained, however, another subject that caught my attention during my study of Marx, namely, his view of history. I wrote a few papers on the subject for Professor Peterson. As one who works in the field of intellectual history, I decided to return to that topic for this brief volume; it is definitely worthy of our attention. In constructing his version of history, Marx regarded the events recorded in the Bible as religious "superstition." But for the Christian, the historical factuality of God's activity as recorded in biblical revelation is fundamental. Often missed is the fact that Cornelius Van Til, in developing his views of epistemology, metaphysics, ontology, and ethics, strongly emphasized the self-attesting Christ of Scripture who is revealed on every page and in every recorded event. A Reformed engagement of, and challenge to, Marx's historiography should focus on exactly this point: is biblical religion superstition or the supernatural lifeblood of human history? This question will orient much of our transcendental analysis of Marx's position.

Obviously, there are a number of individuals who deserve special thanks. I am deeply honored that Nathan Shannon asked me to participate in this series for P&R Publishing. Much appreciation must be expressed to my colleagues at Covenant College. I am especially thankful to James Baird for his many hours of research assistance and his encouragement, and to Associate Professor Cale Horne for permitting me to listen to his fine lectures on Marx in his political science class. I am extremely grateful to Professor Paul Morton, dean of academic programs, who intervened and secured my sabbatical for the fall semester of 2015, and I am also thankful to Associate Professor Alicia Jackson, chair of the Faculty Status Committee, for the sabbatical. Thanks to Jeff Hall, vice president for academic affairs, for supplying financial assistance for the project, and especially to Miriam Mindeman, who offered helpful editorial advice.

1

MARXISM AND THE
MARXIAN TRADITION

The Confusion Surrounding Marx

It is common to hear people say that Karl Marx founded socialism. However, that statement conveys the ignorance that many have about Marx. Even evangelical Christians can get caught up in such an erroneous observation. For many believers, any suggestion of Marx's views on political theory and economics, like the mention of Darwin in discussions about origins, leads to offense. They may reject, without further thought, any statement made by a political figure or party that has any Marxist overtones. Nevertheless, while evangelical Christians must exercise biblical discernment in assessing any system of thought, they are also responsible for fairness and accuracy in their assessment. Investigation shows that Karl Marx and Friedrich Engels viewed neither themselves as the founders of modern socialism, nor socialism as the goal of history. Engels referred to what he and Marx advocated as "scientific socialism"; they declared themselves to be beneficiaries of those whom they referred to as the "utopian socialists": Henri de Saint-Simon (1760–1825), Charles Fourier (1772–1837), and Robert Owen (1771–1858). For Marx, socialism was a means to the end, but not the end itself. In his view of the movement of history, democratic capitalism is replaced by democratic socialism, which is replaced in the end by communism (a classless society).

What also may surprise many evangelical Christians is that Marx saw his view of communism as the most rational outworking of the principles of a democratic society advocated by the French Enlightenment. For Marx, the goal of a democratic society was not the constitutional government established in America. In his judgment, communism was the most consistent application of the trinitarian motto of the Enlightenment: liberty, equality, and fraternity. For Marx, a true republic would be established in the final period of history, [when all human beings would be genuinely free, equal, and united as one people,] and everyone would have everything in common. John Lennon (1940–80) offered a vision of such a world. In his song "Imagine," he invoked the power and reality of imagination from the Romantic era to envision a world without heaven or hell, countries, religion, possessions, greed, or hunger. Instead, he imagined a life in which people truly live in the moment—a life of peace, oneness, brotherhood, and sharing all things in the world.[1] Lennon's narrative reflects the Enlightenment's motto as applied by Marx and Engels in *The Communist Manifesto*—the abolition of religion, countries/nationalities, private property (possessions), and greed, leading to humanity's peaceful sharing of lives of fraternal equality.

A question has emerged over the years as to the authentic understanding of Marx's teaching. Evangelical Christians and the general populace may hastily judge a variety of perspectives

---

1. See http://www.azlyrics.com/lyrics/johnlennon/imagine.html (accessed September 12, 2016). Lyrics by John Lennon (1971).

as Marxist, but scholars have asked whether anyone is truly a follower of Marx's teachings today. Simply put, is there a true Marxist anymore? This question was raised by a member of the analytical school of Marxism, social historian Jon Elster.[2] He raised the question in the 1970s and 1980s, an era when Marxist scholars were avidly debating Karl Marx's philosophy of history. Elster, in fact, argued that significant intellectual and moral components of Marx's thought were no longer plausible. Moreover, he maintained that Marx's most cherished dogmas had been demolished by argument, by history, or by social systems based upon his political philosophy.[3] On this basis, he pointed out that any well-intentioned Marxist in recent times has had to go through quite a transformation in order to hold on to any semblance of Marx's ideas. Elster included himself in this analysis, noting that it was no longer possible for him to embrace all the beliefs that Marx cherished. At the same time, he admitted that some of his own most important notions could be traced back to Marx, such as "the dialectical method and the theory of alienation, exploitation, and class struggle, in a suitably revised and generalized form."[4] This struggle, embodied in Elster's position, has become the focus of those who wish to retain and apply Marx's ideas. Over more than a century, this area of scholarship has come to be recognized as Marxism or the Marxian tradition.

This scholarly struggle among the self-described sympathizers of Marxist ideas extends beyond them. If Elster is correct that it is impossible to hold fully to Marxist ideas today, how can Christians and the general populace accurately interpret politicians, political parties, academics, and economists who have

2. See Jon Elster, *An Introduction to Karl Marx* (Cambridge: Cambridge University Press, 1986), 4; Elster, *Making Sense of Marx* (Cambridge: Cambridge University Press, 1986), xiv.

3. Elster, *An Introduction to Karl Marx*, 4.

4. Ibid.

some connection with Marxist thought? In order for evangelical Christians to make intelligent assessments and reach fair critical judgments, they must (1) understand what Marx actually said on subjects in the context of his day and (2) understand how his teaching has been retooled over time by those who claim that they stand in his tradition. The first chapter of this brief work will meet those conditions—coming to a basic understanding of Marx's position and also mapping out how his position has been amended in the Marxist tradition. This foundation will make it possible to think and speak intelligently about how scholars and politicians have transformed the ideas of Marx to serve their own situations and agendas.[5]

The Beginning of the Marxian Tradition

The Marxian tradition can be traced back to the republication of *The Communist Manifesto* in the nineteenth century. When it was originally published in 1848 as *Manifesto of the Communist Party*, the names Marx and Engels were absent from it. But when it was reissued in Leipzig in 1872, its introduction bore both of their signatures. Later, when a third edition appeared in 1883, Engels, the sole author of its introduction, claimed that the *Manifesto* was essentially the work of Marx. At the twilight of their lives, Marx and Engels were clearly identified as the originators of the foremost document of nineteenth-century socialism, with Engels giving supremacy to Marx. From that time on, Marx would be the focus of any discussion of socialism and its continuing effects.

---

5. Because of the brevity of this work, readers will be provided with numerous names in order to advance their own particular work in the field of Marxism and the Marxian tradition. Each individual mentioned has made important contributions that should be investigated in any continuing study of Marxism. For the sake of good scholarship, these names need to be introduced, although the list is not comprehensive.

Also significant was the document's release in pamphlet form in 1872 by the editors of *Der Volksstaat* (The People's State). This allowed wider distribution, especially among the proletariat. One of those editors, Wilhelm Liebkneckt (1826–1900), had accompanied Marx and Engels to London in 1849. Unlike them, however, Liebkneckt returned to Germany in 1862, where he focused on socialist political activities for workers. Together with August Bebel (1840–1913) and others, he influenced the development of Marxian thought and organized socialist workers' parties on the basis of the *Manifesto*'s militant proletarian agenda. In 1890, this culminated in the Sozialdemokratische Partei Deutschlands (SPD) receiving 1,427,300 votes in the German federal election, more than any other party (though winning only a small number of seats in the Reichstag).[6]

Besides the linking of Marx's name to any discussion of socialism, philosophical discourse became an important characteristic of the Marxist tradition, initiated by Marx's dear friend and colleague, Friedrich Engels (1820–95). Although Marx was not an admirer of the discipline of philosophy, Engels maintained that Marx's thought could be viewed within a philosophical framework. Indeed, after Engels died, "Marxism emerged as a comprehensive philosophy and political practice through which many of the twentieth century's most important social and economic transformations were envisioned and pursued."[7] Philosophers began to critically evaluate Marx's view of ethics, epistemology, and aesthetics, as well as open the door

---

6. See Karl Marx, "Circular Letter to Bebel, Liebknecht, Bracke, and Others: The Manifesto of the Zurich Trio," in Karl Marx and Frederick Engels, *Collected Works*, 50 vols. (New York: International Publishers, 1975–2004), 24:268–69. This collection is hereinafter cited as MECW.

7. Terrell Carver, "Marx and Marxism," in *The History of Continental Philosophy*, ed. Alan D. Schrift, vol. 2, *Nineteenth-Century Philosophy: Revolutionary Responses to the Existing Order*, ed. Alan D. Schrift and Daniel Conway (Durham: Acumen, 2010), 35.

to critically assessing his ideas in the context of economic and social conditions.

If Marxism was to be seen as a comprehensive philosophical system, it was imperative in the expansive age of scientific inquiry for Marxist thinkers to develop a rigorous method for explaining what happens in the world. Engels proposed the method known as *the laws of dialectics*, which was revised by Marxists in the 1920s as *dialectical materialism.* In this construct, [human beings are said to be able to know only the material world that surrounds them.] This injection of scientific positivism does not reject Hegel's influence on Marx.[8] Rather, Marx transformed Hegel's transcendental *Geist* (spirit, mind, consciousness) into a materialistic construct of how society moves dialectically in history. Marx characterized the methods of natural and human production (economic conditions) as the data that formed and transformed society as history progressed, following the dialectical paradigm of thesis-antithesis-synthesis. On the surface, much of Hegel's thought can be placed and analyzed in this triadic pattern; however, nowhere did Hegel use this terminology to describe the dialectical movement of the *Geist*. Rather, Hegel's own depiction of the movement was abstract to concrete, implicit to explicit, in itself to for itself, and potential to actual. Marx's dialectic adapted the same pattern to his materialistic view of the *Geist*. Although Marx affirmed Hegel's criticism of Kant's view of the thing-in-itself (i.e., Hegel held, *contra* Kant, that the thing-in-itself can be known), he maintained that the thing-in-itself is limited to the material world of a politico-economic dialectical movement—in itself to for itself (for us).

[handwritten margin note: production defines society]

8. Scientific positivism was a movement in the mid-nineteenth century that is attributed to the French sociologist and philosopher Auguste Comte (1798–1857). It promoted the observation and measurement of empirical facts without a priori presuppositions, in order to be truly objective about its claims. The only authentic knowledge humans possess, it said, is empirical observation. In this approach to

Orthodox Marxism

Upon Marx's death (1883), as we have seen, Engels took it upon himself to expound and carry on the true teaching of his comrade. Engels has been called the first and greatest representative of "orthodox Marxism,"[9] even though questions have surrounded his interpretation. Others who became identified with this view of Marx's person and work include Karl Kautsky, Georgi Plekhanov, and Daniel De Leon—and later, the Bolsheviks Vladimir Ilyich Lenin and Leon Trotsky. The movement focused upon the politico-sociological economics of Marx in the context of historical determinism (which posits that events are predetermined by various forces). In the year Marx died, Kautsky (1854–1938) founded and edited *Die Neue Zeit*, which became the chief theoretical interpreter of Marxist dogma throughout the world for nearly five decades. It focused on such subjects as historical determinism and democratic equality. At the same time, the Russian orthodox Marxist Plekhanov (1856–1918) focused his attention on the individual's role and activity in history, especially in the context of revolution. He concluded that the great acts performed by an individual in history must always be viewed in the context of the socioeconomic forces of that person's era.

Interestingly, one of the early controversies within orthodox Marxism can be found in both Kautsky and Plekhanov[the question of whether those who are members of a Marxist party should be the impetus of the socialist revolution, or whether that revolution will be an inevitable, spontaneous event because of the politico-economic conditions of society.]Kautsky maintained

(handwritten margin note: Marxist member? or Society as a whole?)

---

science, there is no room for Christian theism.

9. One of the most important discussions of orthodox Marxism is Georg Lukács, *History of Class Consciousness: Studies in Marxist Dialectics*, trans. Rodney Livingstone (Cambridge, MA: MIT Press, 1983), 1–26.

Kautsky:
let it happen

that it is not important to instigate something that is inevitable. On this issue, Sidney Hook points out that Kautsky's orthodox Marxist position seems to be invoking Hegel's maxim from Friedrich Schiller (1759–1805), "Die Weltgeschichte ist das Weltgericht" (world history is the court of world judgment).[10] In the context of quoting Schiller's phrase, Hegel makes a controversial comment: "No people ever suffered wrong; what it suffered, it had merited."[11] Hegel was not trying to justify suffering or persecution; rather, his point was that the act of suffering wrong must be viewed meritoriously as working toward the concrete achievement of freedom for humanity. Specifically, for orthodox Marxism, the suffering of the proletariat merits the inevitable movement to a classless society and humanity's true freedom. Yet, a question remained: could those associated with orthodox Marxism be content with the inevitable? In Russia and beyond its borders, two different answers to the question arose in orthodox Marxism.

In Russia, the Socialist Democratic Party split into two groups in 1903: the Bolsheviks (majority) and the Mensheviks (minority). Lenin (1870–1924) was a key figure among the Bolsheviks, while Julius Martov (1873–1923) was the founder of the Mensheviks, being assisted by the intellectual professor Plekhanov, who set up the theoretical basis for the Mensheviks. The Bolsheviks were intent on seizing political power by revolution, resulting in the dictatorship of the proletariat. The Mensheviks believed that a proletarian revolution should be a gradual outworking of proletarian interests and democratic principles applied and embraced by the entire population of a nation. In 1905, the Mensheviks voiced the position that an

10. See Sidney Hook, *Marx and the Marxists* (Princeton: D. Van Nostrand, 1955), 57.

11. Quote found in Peter C. Hodgson, *Shapes of Freedom: Hegel's Philosophy of World History in Theological Perspective* (Oxford: Oxford University Press, 2012), 168.

initial revolution should be carried out by a coalition of proletarian and liberal bourgeois forces, replacing the czar with a bourgeois, democratic government. On the other hand, the Bolshevik Lenin believed that while a revolution in Russia had to be democratic in nature, it had to lead immediately to a dictatorship of both the proletariat and the peasants. He believed that a moderate path to socialism and communism through an initial bourgeois revolution would never bear the fruit that an initial proletarian revolution would accomplish, because it would get bogged down in power struggles between the bourgeois and the proletariat. Both the Mensheviks and the Bolsheviks claimed to be the sole and rightful heir of Marx. And as the twentieth century progressed, the debate took on additional layers. In particular, was there truly a Leninist-Stalinist version of Marxism, or did Lenin and Stalin represent opposing versions of Marxism? We will return shortly to this question.

Departure from Orthodox Marxism

Meanwhile, other controversies arose. Some thinkers took issue with Engels's formulation of scientific determinism. These Marxists were not convinced that Engels's position, or, for that matter, Marx's own position, did justice to the political and social dynamics of cultural development, especially since his deterministic construct did not seem to match the reality of historical movement (e.g., Eduard Bernstein, Antonio Labriola, Ernst Bloch, and Georg Lukács). By the 1890s, Bernstein (1850–1932) pointed out that the assertion in the *Manifesto* that "the proletariat has no fatherland" was contradicted by the fact that workers at that time had gained political rights and citizenship in Germany. As strong nationalistic pride arose during the nineteenth century, the worker now had equal voting rights, was a fellow owner of the common property of the nation, was a recipient of education, and identified with the fatherland. In fact, as the SPD rose to prominence, the urgency for the German nation to lose its independence for a common government of the world was lost.[12] By 1875, Marx had witnessed the unification of Germany (1871), and he became convinced that the revolution of the proletariat would occur in an industrial European nation, perhaps Germany. The proletariat revolution might begin in one nation, but he foresaw it spreading to other industrial capitalistic states, so he continued to hold that "the proletariat has no fatherland." Plainly, historical reality demanded serious adjustments in the explanation of the advancement of cultural Marxism, adjustments exemplified even in Marx himself. Elster is correct: by the turn of century, Marxism provided clear alterations in the content of its dogmas.

In Russia, the Bolsheviks and the less powerful Mensheviks modified Marx's ideas. First, the Marxist revolution in Russia ran contrary to Marx's projection, since Russia was not an urbanized and industrialized capitalistic state.[13] Second, the Bolsheviks debated the teachings of Marx and how his thought should be applied within their party. Once the Russian Revolution had taken place in March 1917, conflict arose concerning the rights of nations and their self-determination within the Russian Empire. Lenin believed that each national community (e.g., Finland, Poland, Transcaucasia, and the Ukraine) had the right to separate and form its own sovereign nation-state.[14] But Stalin insisted that a new nation should come into existence only by virtue of the proletariat's class struggle. Contrary to Lenin,

12. Eduard Bernstein, "The Most Pressing Problems of Social Democracy" (1890), in *German Essays on Socialism in the Nineteenth Century*, ed. Frank Mecklenburg and Manfred Stassen (New York: Continuum, 1990), 122. This essay comes from Bernstein's *Evolutionary Socialism: A Criticism and Affirmation*.

13. See Karl Marx, *Critique of the Gotha Programme*, in MECW, 24:88–89, 94–95.

14. See Robert C. Tucker, *Stalin as a Revolutionary, 1879–1929: A Study in History and Personality* (New York: W. W. Norton and Company, 1973), 168.

Stalin had no problem with *Soviet* Russia imposing its rule on the smaller nations. Increasingly, this difference between them came to the forefront. Lenin was sympathetic to the construct of a Soviet "federation" of nations in Russia for an interim period for pragmatic reasons, so that the smaller nations would benefit from the larger nation of Russia. However, Lenin still wished that in the long run the smaller nations would become sovereign states, free from Russian authority. On the other hand, Stalin held that Soviet Russia must bring those smaller nations into a permanent "federation" under its control. For Lenin, the dictatorship of the proletariat had to remain just that. Although he was the leader of the movement and became the general secretary of the Bolshevik's Central Committee, he steered clear of viewing himself as a dictator; rather, he viewed himself as needing the continual advice and counsel of those surrounding him (e.g., Trotsky and others). By contrast, in Stalin's rise to power, the Marxist doctrine of the dictatorship of the proletariat converted into rule by himself as dictator; his brand of Marxism evolved into tyranny, autocracy, and totalitarianism, resulting in fear and submission. Indeed, the personal power of Stalin was a far cry from the tenets of orthodox Marxism.

Moving in a somewhat different direction, the Frankfurt School (the Institute for Social Research), which emerged in 1924 for the purpose of stimulating Marxist studies in Germany, attacked Engels's model of materialism (e.g., Carl Grünberg, Max Horkheimer, Theodor W. Adorno, Herbert Marcuse, Walter Benjamin, and Erich Fromm). As new social and philosophical disciplines surfaced in the twentieth century, Marxist scholars were presented with the challenges of interpreting Marx's thought within their context. Indeed, the Frankfurt School transformed Marxism by integrating it with the social sciences. For example, Fromm (1900–1980) and others applied Freud's psychoanalysis to the socioeconomic foundation of Marx's thought. These

Marxists noted that Freud applied psychology to the realm of sociology. As these Frankfurt scholars addressed the institutions of society and the need for institutions to change for the sake of human self-preservation, they studied the process of communal consciousness in order to understand the conditions that would produce societal change. Horkheimer (1895–1973) developed the discipline within philosophy known as critical theory, that is, critical analysis set toward the practical end of liberating and emancipating human beings from conditions of enslavement. Marxist critical theory would express special interest in democratic and egalitarian justice for those who had been oppressed throughout history because of their gender, race, and disability. It also applied a critical analysis to a broad spectrum of disciplines: law, history, sociology, psychology, politics, economics, and aesthetics.

At the same time in France, those in sympathy with Marx reacted critically both to Engels's assessment of Marx and to the character of the Communist Party in the Soviet Union. From 1933 to 1939, the Russian philosopher Alexandre Kojève (1902–68) lectured on Hegel in Paris, attempting to present the German icon through the lenses of Marx's materialism and Heidegger's ontology (theory of being). For this reason, Kojève has been said to have invented Marxist existentialism. Perhaps not surprisingly, Jean-Paul Sartre's *Being and Nothingness* (1943), as well as his essay on *Existentialism as Humanism* (1946), left the French philosophical world wondering if Marx and existentialism were compatible. In these works, Sartre so strongly stressed the independent, free consciousness of being, that critics were forced to doubt whether Sartre's version of existentialism had room for Marx or any critical social theory. Sartre's reply to his critics appeared in *Search for a Method* (1960). He explained that his project was a response to only one question: "Do we have today the means to constitute a structural, historical anthropology?"[15] His answer was that Marxism (not Marx), as a comprehensive philosophy, was the sole system of thought that could fit into his view of human existence and answer that question. By revealing the method of the human understanding (*comprendre*) of experience, Sartre offered a synthesis of Marxism (communal life) and existentialism (human activity) as a means to interpret culture and society as he embraced the historical tension (dialectic) of human existence. Specifically, for Sartre, existentialism provided the ideology for people to become free, and Marxism provided the philosophy for people to make themselves into a communal society. It should also be mentioned that the work of Maurice Merleau-Ponty (1908–61) and Henri Lefebvre (1901–91) appeared in this environment. In fact, Sartre highly respected Lefebvre's work on Marx and Marxism. Carver notes, therefore, that "the common thread [between these Frenchmen] was the application of Marxian notions of social production, class structure, and ideological critique to cultural criticism, social science, and historical research."[16]

A further point related to French Marxism in the 1950s is that many of those who were identified with, or sympathetic to, Marxism welcomed the shocking speech delivered by Nikita Khrushchev (1894–1971) at the twentieth congress of the Communist Party in February 1956. In that speech, Khrushchev, the Party's First Secretary in the Soviet Union, denounced many oppressive policies of the Stalinist era, while exalting Lenin as the true follower of Marx. Many of the French Marxists were already disturbed by Stalin's version of Marxism; in a real sense, Khrushchev's speech gave credence to their concern. Ironically, the French Marxists' praise for Khrushchev was soon transformed

15. Jean-Paul Sartre, *Search for a Method*, trans. Hazel E. Barnes (New York: Vintage Books, 1968), xxxiv. This volume was originally published with Sartre's *Critique of Dialectical Reason* (two volumes in one).

16. Carver, "Marx and Marxism," 50.

into bitter disappointment as he sent Soviet troops into Hungary on November 4, 1956, to suppress a national democratic uprising. They viewed his action as one that followed Stalin's approach.[17] Scholars like Sartre, Merleau-Ponty, Fromm, and the Marxist structuralist Louis Althusser (1918–90) strongly attacked what they viewed as a version of Stalinist Marxism. Sartre urged the French communists not to excuse the Soviet intervention in Hungry:

> Everything considered, the French Communists should be advised not to shout too loudly that the Soviet intervention could not be avoided. For this pious argument carries the most radical condemnation of everything that has been done in Hungary up to now. Tortures, trumped up confessions, fake trials, work camps: these instances of violence are unpardonable in any situation.... The failure of the Stalinists shows in their true light this misery and terror which had no other future than final catastrophe.[18]

Indeed, Sartre, along with Althusser and others, began to advance what became known as the de-Stalinization of Marxism. In particular, Althusser wondered if the disarray, crimes, and errors of Stalin's "dogmatism" could ever restore the integrity of Marxist philosophy, especially his theory of history.[19]

Next door in Italy arose one of the formative figures of Marxism in the first half of the twentieth century, Antonio

17. Interestingly, Dmitri Shostakovich (1906–75) had determined to write his "Symphony No. 11: The Year 1905" in 1955 as a commemoration of the czar's Cossack police unjustly opening fire on protestors at the Winter Palace in St. Petersburg on January 9, 1905. Shostakovich finished the symphony in 1957. It honored not only the fallen in 1905, but apparently also the Hungarian freedom fighters crushed by the Soviet Army in 1956.

18. Jean-Paul Sartre, *The Ghost of Stalin* (1956), trans. Martha H. Fletcher and John R. Kleinschmidt (New York: George Braziller, 1967), 16–17.

19. Louis Althusser, *For Marx* (1965), trans. Ben Brewster (London: Verso,

Gramsci (1891–1937). As a young artist and theater critic, he brought qualities of anxiety and inner dialectical tension to the forefront as he combined imagination and realism in his sympathies for socialism. As the founder of the Communist Party in Rome, he was imprisoned in 1926 under Mussolini's fascist regime and eventually died there. But from within those walls he wrote profusely about his concerns for workers, the peasant class, and industrial capitalism. Although he was sympathetic to Engels's reading of Marx, he did not maintain, as many others did, that Hegel had influenced Marx. Even so, perhaps his foremost contribution to Marxism, influenced by Antonio Labriola (1843–1904), was his assertion that Marx's thought needed to be placed in the context of "praxis" (practice). In his *Prison Notebooks*, his conception of the "philosophy of praxis" held a prominent position. He declared that this was a new, independent, and original conception that synthesized German philosophy, classical English economics, and French political theory and practice. It arrived at a ripe moment in global historical development, promoting an independent and original culture (ideas) in the development of social relations (praxis).[20] Gramsci's view of praxis, along with the postwar work of Pierre Vilar (1906–2003), opened the door to a more precise focus: "Marxism does not view itself primarily as praxis but as praxis informed by scientific theory."[21] Jürgen Habermas sums this up well:

> Within this framework historical materialism can be understood as a theory of society conceived with a practical intent,

2005), 30–31.

20. Antonio Gramsci, *Selections from the Prison Notebooks of Antonio Gramsci*, ed. and trans. Quintin Hoare and Geoffrey Nowell Smith (New York: International Publishers, 2003), 398–400.

21. Georg G. Iggers, *New Directions in European Historiography* (Middletown, CT: Wesleyan University Press, 1975), 145.

which avoids the complementary weaknesses both of traditional politics and of modern social philosophy; it thus unites
the claim to a scientific character with a theoretical structure
referring to praxis.[22]

The Impact of MEGA

World War II brought great changes to the world and thus
to Marxism. In the new political and economic environment,
Marxists were compelled to make creative and fresh philosophical adjustments. Some argued that Engels's construct of
dialectical materialism was out of date, while others thought it
was time to pay much more attention to Marx's philosophy of
history and its connection with Hegel and his later followers.
Becoming prominent in the English-speaking world were two
figures whose works appeared prior to the war, but had last-
ing influence beyond the war, Sidney Hook and Isaiah Berlin
(1909–97). Back in 1927, when the multivolume *Marx-Engels
Gesamtausgabe* (MEGA) began to be published, Hook had
been one of the first scholars to use this source to formulate his
own understanding of Marx. Marx's early works from 1843 to
1847 caught Hook's attention, compelling him to study Marx
in the context of Hegel and the Young Hegelians. According to
Hook, these documents not only demonstrated that Marx was
"drenched" and "nurtured" in Hegel's philosophical tradition,
but also exhibited his critical assessment of the Young Hegelians,
such as David Strauss, Bruno Bauer, Max Stirner, and Ludwig
Feuerbach.[23] In a somewhat complementary direction, Berlin
was one of the formative scholars who thought it best to devote

22. Jürgen Habermas, *Theory and Practice*, trans. John Viertel (Boston: Beacon
Press, 1974), 3.

23. Sidney Hook, *From Hegel to Marx: Studies in the Intellectual Development of
Karl Marx* (Ann Arbor: University of Michigan Press, 1962), 1.

more focus to Marx in his own historical context than to Marx through Engels's spectacles. According to Carver, Berlin contextualized Marx "in a general historical sense involving all kinds of ideas and moments . . . with a wide popular appeal and an interdisciplinary academic profile."[24]

Later in the twentieth century and into the twenty-first century, Bertell Ollman and Norman Levine argued that Marx's thought comprised a complete sociology that had a clear relationship with Hegel's philosophical thought without the mystification of Hegel's *Geist*. Specifically, said Levine, "Marx appropriated Hegel's method, but he rejected Hegel's system."[25] Although first revealed before World War II in 1932 by MEGA, this connection received heightened stimulus in the postwar era by the arrival in print of Marx's *Economic and Philosophic Manuscripts of 1844* and *The German Ideology*. Because of these publications, Carver notes, scholars were now faced with new questions about the "continuity, development, and innovation" within Marx's own thought, and thus less attention was given to Marxism *per se*.[26] Hence, the call went forth: back to Marx. After all, scholars were now in possession of newly published primary sources that needed to be assessed critically. According to Carver, a philosophical focus on these manuscripts, by Marxists as well as by non-Marxists, tended to depoliticize Marx and focus on philosophical categories such as alienation and estrangement, which were carefully debated in characterizing a new Marx: Marx the humanist.[27] Other significant figures who studied such key philosophical concepts in Marx were Herbert

24. Terrell Carver, "The Marxian Tradition," in *The Oxford Handbook of the History of Political Philosophy*, ed. George Klosko (Oxford: Oxford University Press, 2011), 408.

25. See Norman Levine, *Marx's Discourse with Hegel* (Basingstoke: Palgrave Macmillan, 2012), 12, 72, 107, 108, 204, 219, 220, 239, 298, 302, 305.

26. Carver, "Marx and Marxism," 52.

27. Ibid., 53.

Marcuse (1898–1979), Raya Dunayevskaya (1910–87), Shlomo Avineri, and David McLellan. A number of scholars, however, were not convinced this was the way to shape a new Marx, such as Leszek Kolakowski (1927–2009) and Norman Geras (1943–2013). Specifically, Kolakowski called attention to two different emphases in the thought of Engels and Marx that remained relevant in the postwar era. Kolakowski writes: "Whereas Engels . . . believed that man could be explained in terms of natural history and the laws of evolution to which he was subject, and which he was capable of knowing in themselves, Marx's view was that nature as we know it is an extension of man, an organ of practical activity."[28] Kolakowski adopted and applied the praxis language to his understanding of Marx, noting that, for Marx, "human praxis is the true object of our knowledge, which can never free itself from the practical, situational manner in which it is acquired."[29] For Kolakowski and others, attention to the relationship between praxis and knowledge rose above the analysis of popular philosophical categories.

Meanwhile, those in the analytical school of Marxist thought (e.g., G. A. Cohen, Jon Elster, John Roemer, Robert Brenner, and Erik Olin Wright) were responding negatively to the Hegelian interpretation of Marx on the Continent. They strove for a more rigorous, rational understanding of Marx, one formed from their own unique blend of twentieth-century schools of philosophical thought. They combined logical positivism and the philosophy of science of the 1930s with the Oxford school of the philosophy of language (linguistics) in the 1950s, in order to produce a rational construct of individualism and economics. The stimulating work for these Marxists was H. B. Acton's *The Illusion of*

---

28. Leszek Kolakowski, *Main Currents of Marxism: I. The Founders*, trans. P. S. Falla (Oxford: Oxford University Press, 1978), 401.

29. Carver, "Marx and Marxism," 53.

the Epoch: Marxism-Leninism as a Philosophical Creed (1955). Acton had argued that Marx's preface to *Das Kapital* presented an untidy and confusing picture of the forces and relations of production, as well as contradictions in the political struggle for class dominance, referring to Marx's theory as "a philosophical farrago."[30] These analytical Marxists especially endeavored to advance Acton's views in areas of Marx's theory of exploitation dealing with production and exchange.[31] Although he does not explicitly acknowledge Acton's influence on his own understanding of exploitation, Elster does interact in a critical, positive manner with the work of Roemer and Cohen, especially in the field of analytical economics (a technical area of quantitative economics). In terms of production and exchange, Marxism views exploitation in a twofold manner. First, exploitation is morally wrong because it tolerates and generates distributive injustice. Second, in light of this injustice, exploitation provides the justification for protest, rebellion, and revolution.[32]

Since ethics has long been a discipline in the domain of philosophy, it would seem logical that the subject would eventually receive attention in Marxian studies. Indeed, that day did arrive in the 1970s and 1980s, when the subject of justice and morality emerged as a major concern. Examining Marx, one confronts at times his flippant philosophical and religious attitude toward morality and justice, whereas at other times one is struck by his contempt for mere moralizing and superficial notions of fairness.[33] Nevertheless, once Marxists began to concentrate more

---

30. Ibid., 55.

31. See ibid.; H. B. Acton, *The Illusion of the Epoch: Marxism-Leninism as a Philosophical Creed* (London: Cohen and West, 1955), 271.

32. See Elster, *Making Sense of Marx*, 165–233; cf. Elster, *An Introduction to Karl Marx*, 79–102.

33. Terrell Carver, "Karl Marx," in *The Blackwell Guide to the Modern Philosophers: From Descartes to Nietzsche*, ed. Steven M. Emmanuel (Malden: Blackwell Publishers, 2001), 383. Carver's analysis here is based on R. G. Peffer, *Marxism, Morality, and*

intently on the subject of ethics in Marx's thought, their debate revolved chiefly around two questions. First, was Marx to be viewed as an ethical contextualist (i.e., someone holding that morality was controlled by the political and economic interests of the dominating classes in history), thus viewing morality as ideological and relative? Second, was Marx's view of morality a relevant theory of justice that exposed the exploitation and destructiveness of capitalism? As one might expect, in this debate there were proponents on both sides, in addition to those who sought to synthesize the two sides. After all, for Marx, it was imperative to pursue, in an ethical manner, a classless society of political, economic, and social justice.

Perhaps this brief introduction to Marxism and the Marxian tradition is best summarized by David Bakhurst. Placing the legacy of Marx's thought in the realm of philosophy, he argues that two approaches seem to recapitulate Marx's *Weltanschauung* (worldview) holistically. First, there are the Marxists who in some manner trace their analysis of Marx's thought through "theoretical discussions of scientific method, of objectivity, of the relation between natural and social scientific modes of explanation, of necessity and prediction, of the nature of 'false consciousness,'" and so forth. Bakhurst describes this approach as "*scientific realism* that accentuate[s] Marx's confidence in the power of science to render objective reality transparent." Second, there are the Marxists who address their analysis from the position that "Marx takes human praxis to have a world-transforming character." More specifically, "by acting upon reality, human beings change its very nature: the world they confront is no longer brutally physical in kind: it is a 'humanized environment.'" Bakhurst refers to this legacy as "*anthropocentrism*," which emphasizes Marx's claim, not only that the human subject is

---

Social Justice (Princeton: Princeton University Press, 1990).

an active being, but also that the objective world itself must be conceived as 'human sensuous activity, practice.'"[34]

This brief overview of Marxism and the Marxian tradition has aimed to introduce to the reader how Marx's own thought has been further developed and taken in various directions since his death. The multiple threads present a complex picture, requiring careful study in order to distinguish each one clearly and identify its particular characteristics. Elster's assessment seems confirmed: it is doubtful that a true Marxist exists anymore. Anyone who wants to avoid the pitfall of accepting erroneous equivalence between Marx and present-day figures who declare themselves to be in the Marxist tradition must grapple with the scholarly data. Moreover, we must work with primary source material to understand what Marx was saying in his own day and allow Marx to speak for himself, without the presuppositions of others forcing us to reach certain conclusions. Indeed, fair dialogue with Marx begins with the study and comprehension of Marx's own words.

---

34. David Bakhurst, "Marxism," in *Blackwell Companions to Philosophy: A Companion to Epistemology*, ed. Jonathan Dancy and Ernest Sosa (Oxford: Blackwell, 1992), 268–69.

2

A BRIEF SKETCH
OF MARX'S LIFE

From a Jewish Family to a Protestant Family

Who was this man whose name ignited a tradition and an "ism" using his name? Karl Marx was born in Germany; however, he spent more years of his life on British soil, leading some to argue that his thought should be analyzed from within British democratic capitalism and socialism. Marx took up residence in Britain, but had brief sojourns in various cities and countries on the Continent. Moreover, even during those years of residence in Britain, he often traveled to the Continent for conventions and conferences, as well as to meet with party members. A case can be made that he focused his attention on the prospects and conditions for a revolution in his fatherland. Indeed, he never lost contact with the plight of the worker throughout Europe. Perhaps, then, it is best to view Marx's residence in Britain as a matter of convenience in light of the political environment of Europe at the time.

On May 5, 1818, in the historic city of Trier in the Rhineland of southwest Germany, Heinrich and Henrietta Marx welcomed their son Karl into their home. Both parents had a strong Jewish background, which included rabbinical ancestry. This Jewish heritage was an impediment to his father's professional advancement as an attorney when the Rhineland came under Prussian control in 1815. The Prussian government would not allow Jewish attorneys to work as administrative officials. Hence, Heinrich converted to Protestantism around 1819–20, an action at odds with his liberal commitment to Enlightenment thought, which, in turn, had a profound influence on the home education of his son Karl. In 1830, Heinrich permitted Karl to enter the *Gymnasium*. Its director, Johann Heinrich Wyttenbach, a proponent of Enlightenment ideas, continued the liberal, humanistic education that existed in Karl's home. This emphasis was reflected in Karl's essays that were required for graduation from the *Gymnasium* (*Abitur*)—treatises reflecting a moral ideal to serve humanity.

Academic Life

In October 1835, Marx enrolled as a law student at the University of Bonn. There his drinking and getting into brawls unsettled his father, who insisted that his son transfer to the University of Berlin for his second year. Prior to going to Berlin, however, Marx became engaged to Jenny von Westphalen (1814–81), who, being four years older than her future husband, would persevere through seven years of engagement before being married. Meanwhile, at Berlin, a prototype of the modern university, Marx initially directed his attention to writing lyric poetry, romantic ballads, and epigrams, while continuing the study of law. Marx had decided to integrate his study of law with the philosophy of Hegel, which was a waste of time according to his father. In fact, his father was so concerned with his son's direction that he requested that he come home for Easter break in 1838. When Marx arrived at home, he found his father bedridden with tuberculosis. His father died on May 10, 1838, only a few days after Marx returned to Berlin to resume his schooling.

As Marx continued in his studies, he chose to relinquish his father's dream of his making a name in the field of jurisprudence and instead became increasingly interested in Hegel's method of studying philosophy. According to McLellan, Marx's conversion to Hegel was "probably the most important intellectual step of Marx's whole life."[1] Indeed, no matter how critical Marx would become of Hegel, he would confess that his method had its roots in Hegel, who taught at the University of Berlin from 1818 until his death in 1831. Although Hegel was gone before Marx's arrival, the young student became fascinated with Eduard Gans (1798–1839), who was a legal historian and an advocate of Hegelian thought at the University. When Gans died unexpectedly of a stroke in 1839, Marx turned his focus to "a loosely knit group of philosophers, theologians, and freelance intellectuals, contemporaries called the Young Hegelians."[2] His doctoral dissertation on Epicurus demonstrated the influence of Hegel and the young Hegelian Bruno Bauer (1809–82), his teacher and friend. Marx traced the development of atomism from Democritus's abstract view to Epicurus's concrete view, arguing that it reached its apex in the dialectical progress of self-consciousness. When Marx was dropped from the University of Berlin's rolls for going beyond four years to receive his doctorate, the University of Jena received his dissertation, and his doctorate was bestowed on April 15, 1841.

1. David McLellan, *Karl Marx: His Life and Thought* (New York: Harper & Row, 1973), 28.
2. Jonathan Sperber, *Karl Marx: A Nineteenth-Century Life* (New York: Liveright Publishing, 2013), 60.

After returning to Trier for six weeks, he moved to Bonn in order to pursue an academic career. The German academic system required another step towards this vocation—a post-doctorate dissertation known as a *Habilitationsschrift*. Marx's study expanded upon his previous study, examining Epicurean, Stoic, and skeptical philosophy. In this dissertation, his commitment to Enlightenment rationalism is clearly in the forefront when he considers the existence of God. It is also said that for the first time he articulated his notions of the suppression of philosophy and concern about praxis.[3] Marx was at this point becoming known as a militant atheist, and, when Bauer was denied promotion from lecturer to a permanent academic position at the University of Bonn because of his own atheism, Marx realized that his own career in academics would not be forthcoming. So he made a move to journalism, becoming closely associated with Arnold Ruge (1802–80), who was also estranged from university teaching. In this atmosphere, Marx became increasingly sensitive to the political landscape as he applied Hegel's philosophy to liberal democratic ideas.[4]

Initial Involvement in Journalism

Because of the stifling academic atmosphere in Bonn, Marx moved in 1842 to Cologne, where he enjoyed champagne and personal interaction in the Hegel clubs. But this atmosphere grew dull to him, so he returned to Bonn in order to be close to Bauer. But he still made frequent visits to Cologne, attracted by its political and philosophical tone. In fact, according to McLellan, his visits there led to "involvement in the city's liberal opposition movement, an involvement in practical politics that eventually

3. See McLellan, *Karl Marx*, 41.
4. Ibid., 44.

led to his breaking with the Young Hegelians and taking over the editorship of the *Rheinische Zeitung*."[5] The paper was begun by persons in the Cologne Circle who had bought the bankrupt *Rheinische Allgemeine Zeitung*. Such key figures as Georg Jung and Moses Hess (1812–75) convinced others who were sympathetic to those suffering from perceived economic and social injustices to buy the paper in order to get their message before the public. Jung and Hess, impressed with Marx's revolutionary spirit and intellectual abilities, made him part of the editorial staff of the paper.

With Marx on board, the *Rheinische Zeitung* soon tripled in circulation and became nationally known. Articles were written by those associated with communism and socialism, and the paper would not shy away from discussing freedom of the press, constitutional monarchy, moral theory, socioeconomic conditions, political grievances, free trade, property rights, equal judicial rights, and the relationship between civil freedom and equality. When the Rhineland Parliament dealt with the question of whether people who collected wood that had fallen in the forest were guilty of theft, Marx for the first time took an interest in economic questions, which led him "from pure politics to economic relationships and so to socialism."[6] Specifically, the government decided that deadwood in the forest did not belong to everyone, so that the poor could not freely pick it up and use it to secure warmth in winter. Marx's increased awareness of the socioeconomic plight of the lower classes helped to drive him toward communism. He had already been exposed by Eduard Gans to the fundamental theories of communism from Henri de Saint-Simon, including the crucial idea of abolishing private property and turning land over to common ownership.

5. Ibid., 45.
6. Ibid., 57 (letter from Engels to R. Fischer).

Although Marx's editorial directive was to moderate the tone of the paper, he still allowed sarcasm and a confrontational attitude to characterize its articles. This arrogance did not endear the paper to the Prussian government, and so, after too many of the articles crossed the line in criticizing the government, its censors shut down the paper. The last issue was published on March 31, 1843, but Marx had already resigned on March 17 in protest of the censorship. For Marx, it was becoming increasingly challenging to stay in Germany.

After the shutdown of the *Rheinische Zeitung* in the spring of 1843, Marx quickly moved to assist Arnold Ruge in establishing the *Deutsch-Französische Jahrbücher*, a journal dedicated to promoting the ideas of intellectuals committed to a new wave of radical democratic thought. The journal was published in Zurich by Julius Fröbel (1803–93), a professor of mineralogy who was dedicated to the radical interpretation of the Enlightenment's ideals of liberty, equality, and fraternity. Marx received a fine salary with the job, and so he and Jenny finally got married on June 19, 1843. They settled in Kreuznach and then moved to Paris in October 1843, where they remained for a year and a half. Ruge and Hess had already preceded Marx to Paris, which had become a cradle for intellectual liberalism. There Marx interacted with German and French intellectuals, a number of whom he had not previously known. Sperber notes that Marx's thought during this period grew to include "his redefinition of the future ideal regime as communist; his investigation of the works of the major economists of the day and incorporation of their findings into his new worldview; his identification of the working class as the vehicle for political transformation; and his restatement of Feuerbach's version of Young Hegelians, to put an emphasis on the labor process."[7]

7. Sperber, *Karl Marx*, 119.

Although Marx's Paris experience brought these elements into his thought, the *Deutsch-Französische Jahrbücher* did not survive its initial double issue of articles, mainly by German authors. As much as Marx focused his energy on the journal, he could not get French authors to write for it, and the publication's financial condition deteriorated to the point where no revival was possible. Even so, Marx contributed two articles: "Contribution to the Critique of Hegel's Philosophy of Law" and "On the Jewish Question." In the former, Marx critiqued the societal production of religion, making his famous statement that religion is the "opium of the people." In the latter, Marx's demeaning criticism of Judaism earned the label of anti-Semitism.

Marx Meets Engels

The reports of Marx's first meeting with Friedrich Engels in November 1842 characterize it as "frosty" and "cold."[8] Although Marx had published material by Engels in the *Rheinische Zeitung*, he showed no serious interest in Engels. Perhaps Marx gave Engels the cold shoulder because he looked at the *Freien*— a club in Berlin, of which Engels was a charter member—as immature, arrogant, politically romantic, and intellectually shallow. Marx's attitude changed, however, in November 1843, when Engels submitted "Outlines of a Critique of Political Economy" to the *Deutsch-Französische Jahrbücher*. This piece made a profound impression on Marx. Engels provided great insight into the issues of private propriety, competition, class struggle, and the oppression of workers. Particularly noteworthy was Engels's argument for the elimination of private property, which would become a keystone of communism. In

8. Terrell Carver, *Marx and Engels: The Intellectual Relationship* (Bloomington: Indiana University Press, 1983), 1–2, 25.

Marx's eyes, Engels had advanced beyond Hegel to meet the challenges of post-Enlightenment Europe, applying social theory to its politico-economic environment. Still, their lifetime friendship was not launched until their personal meeting in late August 1844, when they spent ten days together in Paris. By this point, Marx had become part of the editorial staff of the new *Vorwärts*, in which his article on the revolt of the Silesian weavers had appeared in July. The article did not sit well with the Prussian government, which urged the French authorities to take action. The French government promptly shut down the *Vorwärts* presses, and Marx moved on to Brussels in 1845, where he remained for three years.

Although Belgium was surpassing France with its number of political refugees and was increasingly becoming known for free expression, the Prussian government pressured the Belgian government to deny Marx residence. Marx was able to receive a home permit by promising not to be involved in political activity. Although his activity was more reserved in Brussels, Marx continued to pay attention to political organizations throughout Europe that supported communism. In fact, he and Engels founded a Communist Committee of Correspondence in 1846, and in the early part of 1847 they joined what remained of the League of the Just in London. Furthermore, in December 1847 the Communist League held a congressional meeting for its delegates in London. Both Marx and Engels attended, and they left that meeting with the task of writing a manifesto declaring the basic position of the League. After a number of drafts, including a catechism written by Engels, entitled "Principles of Communism," Engels declared that the final edition of *The Communist Manifesto* was "essentially Marx's work." It was published in London in February 1848.

When a revolution erupted in the streets of Paris in 1848 and spread to other nations in Europe, the Belgian government, like the French government, grew nervous about organizations with republican ideas. In Belgium, one such group was the Brussels Democratic Association, of which Marx was vice president. When Marx's mother sent him inheritance money, the Belgian police mistakenly thought he would use it to fund a revolution in their country. Marx was placed in jail, and on March 3, 1848, he and his family were forced to exit the country. They returned to Paris, where they discovered that many individuals whom Marx and Engels had discipled were in leadership positions in the government. Meanwhile, many German states had begun to loosen restrictions on freedom. Marx, Engels, and others saw an opportunity to move back to Germany and take advantage of this new situation. On April 11, 1848, Marx again set up residence in Cologne with the hope of editing a newspaper. His goal was achieved quickly, as funding had already been raised for the start of the *Neue Rheinische Zeitung*. As chief editor, Marx became critical of the political radicals who compromised their agenda with ideas from political moderates. According to Engels, the newspaper and its editor had two primary objectives: a single, indivisible German republic (against Prussia) and an invasion to overthrow the Russian czar in order to bring liberation to Poland, which at the time was divided between Russia, Austria, and Prussia. The paper stood for "universal suffrage, direct elections, the abolition of all feudal dues and charges, the establishment of a state banking system, and the admission of state responsibility for unemployment."[9] In response to this agenda, the Prussian authorities attempted to get Marx convicted of press violations, but they failed. After that, they waited for another opportunity to get rid of him. In May 1849, they used a false report that he was mounting an insurrection in order to expel Marx. He left with his family and Engels, never to live again in the Rhineland. They moved to Paris for three months and then on to England.

9. McLellan, *Marx*, 201.

Marx Resides in London

In London, Marx faced the financial challenge of supporting his family. Nevertheless, he immediately became active in political affairs. Within a year, he and Engels joined the Universal Society of Communist Revolutionaries, whose goal was to overthrow all privileged classes in order to establish the dictatorship of the proletariat. Although the British government was approached by the Prussian and Austrian governments about Marx, Engels, and others, British law protected the refugees as long as they presented no threat to the Queen and British government. After all, as a result of the revolutions of 1848, London had welcomed many European refugees, including those from Germany.

As Marx took up residence in London, he wanted to capitalize on the revolutions of 1848. After the defeat of democratic and socialist revolutions throughout Europe, Marx believed that a revolutionary eruption of the proletariat was now needed. His inflammatory rhetoric in public and private discourse became more pronounced. He supported the workers organizing themselves independently from the bourgeoisie in order to achieve revolution. Marx also declared that those who were the wealthiest should be taxed so much that their capital would be extinguished. Furthermore, he voiced the view that the initial democratic process should move toward the all-inclusive centralization of the state. Marx came to advocate, along with Engels, that workers had to find their own independent candidates to run in elections against bourgeois candidates. The defeat of the 1848 revolutions needed rectification, and so Marx moved to a more radical agenda. His plan could be clearly perceived in the title of his new journal, *Neue Rheinische Zeitung—Politisch-Oekonomisch Revue*, which would be published out of Hamburg. The title conveys the continuation of his journal in

Cologne, suggesting a politico-economic focus. Publication commenced in March 1850 and ended in November 1850. Although the journal contained significant articles by Marx, Engels, and others, the content was too intellectually challenging. In addition, its politico-economic discussions seemed ignorant of the science of those disciplines. Marx responded by getting admittance to the British Museum in June 1850, where he became a serious reader of the *Economist*. For a time, he withdrew from personal involvement in political activism and studied in the Museum from nine in the morning until seven in the evening.

Marx began a period of reflection. He realized that a democratic socialist revolution would have difficulty achieving victory, given the political and economic conditions. Also, he recognized that tensions existed within the movement that prevented unified action. Marx began to argue that a simple workers' revolt would not lead to a revolution. Rather, a revolution would only occur with the dawn of a "cyclical capitalist economic crisis."[10] That is, an economic crisis in capitalism would bring about a workers' revolution, not the other way around. This change in his position on revolution would become a defining factor in his thought. Hence, Marx attempted to analyze economic conditions throughout Europe in order to assess when and where an economic crisis would lead to a revolution. In the 1850s, his eyes focused on France.

In this period, economic hardship plagued the Marx family in London. Income from the *Revue* did not meet their expenses, and Marx could not pay the rent on an apartment in the slum district of Soho. He constantly wrote IOUs, and creditors eventually refused any more loans. At the same time, Marx's mother and Jenny's family members refused to provide further financial

10. Sperber, *Karl Marx*, 274.

assistance. Marx and Engels considered moving to New York, but could not raise the money for a one-way trip. Engels pleaded with his wealthy parents in Manchester, England, for money, claiming that he was no longer a communist, but a capitalist. His parents were not convinced of the conversion, but circumstances worked in his favor. When Engels was given permission to inspect his father's books, he noticed that "his father's business partners, the Ermen brothers, were cheating him."[11] In response to this discovery, Engels's father hired him and provided him with a fine income. Engels immediately came to the aid of Marx, bringing some financial relief, although he could not remove all the debt. Tragically, Karl and Jenny lost two children within a year and a half: Heinrich Guido on November 19, 1850, and Franziska on April 14, 1852. Also, there is strong evidence that Lenchen Demuth, who was the Marx family's servant, bore an illegitimate son (Henry Fredrick) to Marx on June 23, 1851, though at the time the unmarried Engels claimed that child was his.

Adversity followed Marx and his family through the rest of the 1850s. The deaths of Heinrich and Franziska were followed by the devastating losses of their eight-year-old son Edgar on April 6, 1855, and a child who was stillborn in July 1857.

On the London scene during the early 1850s, Marx took a low profile with respect to political activism because of tensions among the refugees there. Moreover, he was preoccupied with his financial condition, his own health issues, the suffering that Jenny endured, and the distressing living conditions in Soho. Still, after enduring the financial strains of 1852, he would see gradual improvement in the years that followed. He became a London correspondent for the *New York Daily Tribune* in 1852, and this continued through March 1862.[12] He received payment

11. Ibid., 260.
12. McLellan notes: "In all the *Tribune* published 487 articles from Marx, 350

that increased each year through October 1856. It decreased in November 1856, but he was able to compensate for some of the loss by serving as a correspondent for the *Neue Oder-Zeitung* and by becoming involved with Engels in publishing articles for *The New American Cyclopaedia*. In 1856, Jenny received two inheritances, one from an uncle in Scotland and the other from her mother, which enabled the family to leave Soho and rent a three-story house on the border of the Hampstead Heath section of London. By 1859, Marx's financial condition had become stable and secure. Also, in the midst of all the Marxes' struggle and pain during that decade, one joyful event stands out: the birth and survival of their daughter Eleanor on January 17, 1855.

Renewed Political Activism

By 1859, Marx's concern for events in Europe had stimulated his interest in political activism once again. A war that is little known today, the Italian War of 1859, particularly intrigued him. Although Marx had followed the events surrounding the Crimean War from 1853 to 1856, his life was more stable by 1859, so that he could study and become involved in the political rhetoric surrounding this invasion by Napoleon III (1808–73) of the Austrian provinces in northern Italy. He and Engels were opposed to Napoleon III and hoped that a number of German states would come to the aid of Austria against France. They reasoned that in order to protect the western states of Germany, France needed to be defeated. Furthermore, in the eyes of Marx, Napoleon III and the Russian czar were collaborating against the Austrian Empire. Seeing this vulnerability of Europe prompted Marx to reassess the importance of his engaging once

---

written by him, 125 written by Engels (mostly on military matters) and twelve written in collaboration" (*Marx*, 287).

again publicly in the communist movement. He became more visibly active with the German refugees in London, which laid the groundwork for his involvement later in the International Working Men's Association. Meanwhile, because of his loss of employment by the *Tribune*, Marx's financial woes resurfaced from 1862 to 1864. It took two inheritances to bring the Marxes relief in 1864—one from Marx's mother, and the other from his dear friend Wilhelm Wolf (1809–64), who died while living in Manchester. In these first years of the 1860s, poverty and ill health had led Marx once again to recede from political activism. He suffered from painful growths that appeared throughout his body, and which, on occasion, had to be removed. With the funds that they received from the inheritances, the Marx family moved to an upscale neighborhood in North London, and he resumed his political involvement.

Although he declined to be editor since he was not a Prussian citizen, Marx became deeply involved in "the first daily socialist paper in Germany, the *Social Democrat*, which started appearing in Berlin at the beginning of 1865."[13] Also, in late 1864 Marx participated in the founding of the International Working Men's Association (IWMA) in London. As a prominent member of the organizing committee, he drafted a manifesto for the new organization. But while the organization echoed many ideas that Marx advocated, not everyone agreed on all issues. For example, Marx strongly supported Poland's liberation from the tyranny of Russia, whereas the French delegation did not support the "political reconstruction of Poland." Nevertheless, when the First Congress met in Geneva in September 1866, the members united on a number of issues: "a shorter workday, limitations on women and children's labor, the replacement of indirect with direct taxation, an international inquiry into workplace conditions—and

13. Sperber, *Karl Marx*, 355.

the endorsement of producers' cooperatives and trade unions."[14] The organization mobilized to fund unionists who were striking and to provide democratic candidates for elections.

As Marx became strongly involved in the IWMA, he could not overlook the signs of a new potential democratic revolution, a political situation unmatched since the revolutions of 1848. Demonstrations, turbulence, uprisings, strikes, and mass meetings took place in many European nations. Moreover, in June 1866, Prussia, under the leadership of Bismarck, went to war with Austria. Marx and Engels supported Austria and were surprised when Prussia defeated Austria in six weeks. With this victory, Bismarck dissolved the German Confederation and unified the German states. Bismarck was not done; in 1870, the new Prussia went to war with France, humiliating the French army and capturing Napoleon III. Interestingly, Marx and Engels supported Prussia in this; for them, the aggressive and dictatorial French emperor had to be suppressed. As the emperor was in prison, a new government, the French National Assembly, was established in Versailles, while in March 1871 radicals in Paris established their own government, known as the Paris "Commune." The Versailles government viewed the Commune as a communist entity led by Marx, even though he had little connection with it. To be sure, Marx communicated his thoughts about the Commune in a speech, "The Civil War in France," before the General Council of the IWMA on May 30, 1871. In addition, the first volume of his *Das Kapital* had already been published in Hamburg in 1867.

The false publicity surrounding Marx's connection with the Commune brought him, perhaps more than ever, to the attention of socialists throughout Europe. He was interviewed by the *New York World*, and his biography appeared in the November

14. Ibid., 358.

11, 1871, issue of Paris's *Illustrated News* and was reprinted in newspapers in England, Spain, Italy, Germany, and America. That same year, the Franco-Prussian war had prevented the IWMA from holding its annual congress. After the IWMA had gained strength and influence from 1867 to 1869, the war led some to be concerned about whether nationalistic interests would break down the cooperative, international flavor of the group. An even greater concern for many was the difference of philosophy between Marx and the anarchist Mikhail Bakunin (1814–76). Marx aimed for control, and, with the support of the General Council, he maneuvered to have The Hague chosen for the congress meeting in September 1872. Those more sympathetic to Marx's agenda came from northern Europe, whereas those in sympathy with Bakunin's agenda lived in nations closer to the Mediterranean. Marx was hopeful that fewer delegates of Bakunin's persuasion would attend a meeting in The Hague. With this maneuvering, Marx was able to gain control of the meeting and to get Bakunin, who did not attend, ousted from the IWMA. Furthermore, Marx got the seat of the General Council moved to New York, and the organization dissolved in Philadelphia in 1876. While this action removed the central seat from continental Europe, it left the IWMA's center of gravity in Marx's London home. Many affiliates from European nations refused to comply with this action. Marx's actions were purposeful because he believed that having rival factions within the IWMA would prevent the kind of unity needed for revolutionary success.

Clearly, the erosion of the IWMA was set in place, and then further serious health issues arose for Marx in 1873, leaving him with even less capacity to give his attention to the organization. He did not cease political activity, but his doctor limited him to a daily schedule of writing (four hours per day) and encouraged him to travel to places that would be more therapeutic. Although his health improved to some degree, he settled more into the role of "advisor and observer" of political activity.[15] In the last half of the 1870s and into the early 1880s, he focused on the destiny of the Ottoman Empire, the economic and labor turmoil throughout Europe and North America, the economic struggles of the farmers in England, the effects of imperialism, and the efforts of the Russians to conspire their way to prominence. Once again in 1881, his health issues reemerged and his doctors recommended that he move to a warmer climate. He traveled much to find relief, only to return to London and die in his study on March 14, 1883. Sadly, his wife had died of cancer on December 2, 1881, and his eldest daughter had died of bladder cancer on January 11, 1883.

15. Ibid., 519.

3

MARX'S PHILOSOPHY
OF HISTORY

Why History?

What is the best pathway to take in order to engage with Marx's thought? The answer to that question would differ among the various scholars who investigate his ideas. Having their own particular interests—such as economics, political theory, social theory, class warfare, the division of labor, and religion—scholars understandably focus on what is important to them. For our purposes, however, the question concerns how we may understand and contend with the organic and coherent nature of Marx's thought. Indeed, one response seems most appropriate for the Christian. Marx lived in a century when the secularization of the West, linked to the Enlightenment's attack on orthodox Christianity, was a central focus in academic and ecclesiastical circles. The Enlightenment had placed Christian theism and the integrity of the biblical word on trial, with attacks based on the autonomous power of human reason and the empirical analysis of human experience.

The center of Enlightenment thinkers' criticism was their condemnation of belief in a sovereign and transcendent God whose providential activity operated in every event of history. Embracing the premise that the God of the Bible cannot act in history, they rejected the traditional domains of natural and special revelation. Moreover, they annulled the organic, coherent, and integrative quality of God's revelatory activity. Clearly, *nothing is more fundamental to the Christian apologetic than the defense of God's providential activity in history.*[1] For this reason, when grappling with Marx or any other children of the Enlightenment, support from the following thinkers is paramount: Geerhardus Vos (1862–1949) with respect to the biblical text, and Cornelius Van Til (1895–1987) with respect to philosophical apologetics.

Marx was a friendly recipient of the changing dynamics of historiography from the Enlightenment. He fully embraced its naturalistic and secular nuances (e.g., the perspective of Rousseau) positioned against a Christian view of history. Furthermore, Marx arrived upon the German academic scene when historicism, associated with the historiography of Johann Gottfried Herder (1744–1803) and Georg Wilhelm Friedrich Hegel's (1770–1831) version of dialectical historiography, had gained relative credence. Such things as the attention to national character and the development of historical change from Herder, as well as the dialectical movement of history from Hegel, received support in Marx's historiography. From the Enlightenment and these two German figures, the discipline of history became the center of an organic interpretation and understanding of human life and existence. It is somewhat surprising that this component in Marx's thought virtually escaped the attention of many Marxian scholars until multiple

---

1. See Westminster Confession of Faith, 5.1–7.

volumes were added to the publication of the Marx-Engels works (MEGA) in the 1930s. It would take decades for Marxian academicians to grasp the importance of history—its organic, holistic, foundational position—in Marx's thought. In the discipline of history, Marx and Christian theism meet with contrasting worldviews. In this chapter, we will investigate various components of the road taken by Marx and Marxian scholars in this regard.

Marx's Philosophy of History Emerges

As scholars studied the Marx-Engels works (MEGA), philosophy of history increasingly became a focus of attention in the 1970s, stimulated most notably by *Karl Marx's Theory of History*, by G. A. Cohen.[2] In the second edition of his book, which appeared in 2000, Cohen declared that his analytical method was the only legitimate way to understand Marx's theory of history. Of course, his brash claim failed to receive universal consent. Dissent was expressed at a conference held in 2003 by the Marxism Specialist Group of the UK Political Studies Association, when various Marxist scholars revisited Cohen's influential work. Cohen had defended "an old-fashioned historical materialism . . . in which history is, fundamentally, the growth of human productive power, and forms of society rise and fall according as they enable or impede that growth."[3] Scholars at the conference scrutinized and criticized Cohen's analytical method in such areas as his "overreliance on human rationality as a driving mechanism" (Paul Nolan, Alan

---

2. G. A. Cohen, *Karl Marx's Theory of History: A Defense* (Princeton: Princeton University Press, 1978). Cf. also William H. Shaw, *Marx's Theory of History* (Stanford: Stanford University Press, 1978); Melvin Rader, *Marx's Interpretation of History* (New York: Oxford University Press, 1979).

3. Cohen, *Karl Marx's Theory of History*, x.

Carling), his failure to deal much with the relationship between base and superstructure or the connections between the state and history (Paul Wetherly), his interpretation of the abolition of the division of labor (Renzo Llorente), and his understanding of exchange-value and use-value (Alex Callinicos).[4] From this reaction, it seems that Cohen cannot claim to be the sovereign interpreter of Marx's theory of history.

Although Marx's theory of history became a central focus in the 1970s and 1980s, the subject had, of course, been previously explored in the Marxian tradition. Specifically, Engels made his own contribution. In *Socialism: Utopian and Scientific* (1880), he portrayed Marx as the foremost spokesman of the materialist interpretation of history. Later, within the debate on interpreting Marx after World War I, Lukács pleaded in his 1922 edition of *History and Class Consciousness* that Marxists had to return to a true view of Marx. The key, according to Lukács, was to rediscover the ontological foundation of Marx's thought, that is, the ontological objectivity of nature, including the nature of human beings. In order to achieve this, a method had to be employed that matched nature and thus was thoroughly historical.

Following Lukács's premise closely, Louis Althusser (1918–90) carefully investigated Marx's writings and made his contribution to Marx's theory of history in the 1960s. Integrating Marx into French structuralism, Althusser presented a caricature that contrasted the early and later Marx: he referred to the early Marx as an expounder of immature humanism, and the later Marx as the mature and rigorously scientific Marx—stating that the transition to the later Marx began when he wrote "Theses on Feuerbach" and (with Engels) *The German Ideology* in 1845–46

---

4. The presentations at that conference are in *Science & Society*, 70, 2 (April 2006). In that volume, an overview is presented by Alan Carling and Paul Wetherly, "Introduction: Rethinking Marx and History," 146–54.

and was completed in 1857. Althusser's position became a focal point of analysis and criticism during the 1970s and 1980s as Marxist scholars focused more intently on *The German Ideology*, "Theses on Feuerbach," *Economic and Philosophic Manuscripts of 1844*, *The Communist Manifesto*, *Grundrisse*, the preface to *A Contribution to the Critique of Political Economy*, and sections of *Capital*. In order to present a synopsis of Marx's theory of history, I have opted to work, not through the vast amount of scholarship on these works, but through crucial sections in these primary sources.[5]

Marx's Materialist Interpretation of History

Although it is vital to recognize an important progression in the thought of Marx, it is equally necessary to allow Marx to convey this progression. In his preface to *A Contribution to the Critique of Political Economy* (1859), Marx points out that his materialist interpretation of history went back to the years 1842–44, when he edited the *Rheinische Zeitung* in Cologne.[6] At that time, Marx recounted the horrid living conditions of the Moselle's winegrowers, blaming their state of affairs on Prussia. In view of this poverty, Marx became further infuriated as he observed the judicial proceedings of the Rhenish Landtag with respect to the peasants' taking of wood from open land, and the government's sudden parceling of open land to private owners. Marx notes that the Moselle event stimulated his first preoccupation with economic questions. Prior to this awakening, he had

5. Since, in my judgment, the discussion of Marx's theory of history has not advanced far beyond the deliberations in the 1980s, Gregor McLennan's *Marxism and the Methodologies of History* (New York: Verso, 1981) remains a fine introduction to the history of scholarly interpretation of Marx's theory of history.

6. See Karl Marx, preface to *A Contribution to the Critique of Political Economy*, in MECW, 29:261.

been focused on law, philosophy, and history. The challenge for him now lay in determining how economics was to be integrated into these disciplines. He believed the proper path began with a critical examination of Hegel's *Philosophy of Right*. As a result of this investigation, he made the classic statement of his materialistic conception of history: the preface of his *A Contribution to the Critique of Political Economy*. His study disclosed that neither the origin and formation of law in a civil society nor the origin and formation of the state in a civil society will be found in an *a priori* conception of law or the state. Neither will it be found in the progressive evolution of the human mind, as it applies law and the formation of the state to the world in which it exists. Rather, Marx's conclusion is that all legal relations and forms of the state "originate in the material conditions of life, the totality of which Hegel . . . embraces within the term 'civil society.'"[7] In other words, the sum total of the relations of production (social structures that regulate the relation between humans and the production of goods) constitutes the economic structure of society, which, in turn, is the real foundation for law and politics within a given society.

Marx believed, therefore, that the economic structure of society is the base or foundation (*Grundrisse*) of society's superstructure. For Marx, once humans passed beyond a classless primitive society, humanity's relations of production became the economic base upon which society was built. Production, distribution, exchange, and consumption are implicit in this economic structure of society, and these components are interconnected, as well as interdependent. As Marx carried out his empirical investigation of history, he observed that changes have occurred in the base and the superstructure, with these alterations taking place a number of times through the centuries.

7. Ibid., 262.

How does this happen? According to Marx, it happens when "the material productive forces of society [e.g., labor power, techniques of labor, organization of the labor force] come in conflict with the existing relations of production," so that the latter is confined or restrained.[8] This "social revolution" then begins a new era in the modes of production (everything that goes into the production of the necessities of life). For Marx, this uprising has the effect of changing the economic foundations, while at the same time transforming the superstructure. In this analysis of history, the historian's task is to reveal the conflicts between the social productive forces and the relations of production in order to show the emergence of the new modes of production. Indeed, in Marx's view, the materialist interpretation of history has established that humanity's social existence determines humanity's consciousness.[9] Simply put, the economic relationships of human beings produce the necessities of life, which are the foundation of history, namely, the formation of society, human laws, and the state.

History as the Revealer of Truth

Without reaching a consensus, Marxist scholars have debated at great length whether the base-and-superstructure model proves that Marx was an economic determinist.[10] Space does not permit me to shed much light on this debate, but a few remarks

8. Ibid., 263.

9. Ibid. Cf. Karl Marx and Friedrich Engels, *The German Ideology*, in MECW, 5:44: "Consciousness is . . . from the very beginning a social product."

10. There are three main positions supported by scholars: (1) the fundamentalist position (see Shaw, *Marx's Theory of History*), (2) the dialectical position (Engels), and (3) the organic position (see Rader, *Marx's Interpretation of History*). The fundamentalist position understands Marx's position as economic determinism. It interprets Marx as saying that there is an exclusively one-way, causal determinism from base (the economic system) to superstructure. But the dialectical

may be helpful. First, we must keep in mind that in the preface to his *Contribution to the Critique of Political Economy*, Marx states that consciousness is a social product. This social product, according to Marx, is the economically productive activity of living individuals. This view is foundational to a natural or materialist interpretation of history, as opposed to an intellectual interpretation of history. Second, in this passage Marx leaves us with a determinist element that is ambiguous. For this reason, any investigation of an historical mode of production requires a careful analysis of the base and superstructure, in abstract to concrete form, noting that there is an interaction between them. Third, it seems that Marx considers an organic relationship of base and superstructure to characterize every society in history, whether primitive (e.g., the family) or highly scientific and industrial (e.g., capitalism). Finally, we must emphasize that the economic productivity of society is dependent upon living individuals.

According to Marx, then, history is the study of practical human activity (praxis); it is the study of "living human individuals." "Once the *world beyond the truth* has disappeared," the task of history "is to establish the *truth of this world*."[11] In this perspective, the truth of history is not found in a mechanical and abstract analysis of "dead facts," which the empiricist does, nor is the truth of history found in imagining the transcendent movement of consciousness as it comes to expression in imagined subjects, which the idealist does. Rather, to Marx, the truth of

---

position interprets Marx as saying that there is a dialectical interaction between the base and the superstructure, not a one-way, causal relationship. Last, the organic position states that there is an organic wholeness to the entire model of base and superstructure. Such a position aims to avoid all views of reductionism in Marx's position, while at the same time advocating the concrete position of Marx's economic materialism.

11. Karl Marx, *Contribution to the Critique of Hegel's Philosophy of Law: Introduction*, in MECW, 3:176.

history begins with the concrete activity of human beings living in the material world. In short, humanity makes history. What is truly there every day is human beings living in the process of development. Furthermore, this formulation and understanding of history replaces the illusions of religion, taking its place as the authentic revealer of truth.

Marx not only attacks religion, but also criticizes the primacy of philosophy in verifying authentic knowledge (epistemology). Indeed, according to Marx's theory of history, philosophy serves history in the revelation of truth. The task of philosophy is not to provide an abstract theory of knowing truth; rather, the task of philosophy is to unfold the self-alienation of human activity in its secular and material form.[12] Hence, Marx's theory of history will not permit philosophy to function as an independent branch of knowledge. After all, philosophy has "only *interpreted* the world." For Marx, if philosophy is to have any relevance at all, it must serve and adopt his position on real history; in accordance with Feuerbach's (1804–72) famous quip, human activity in time and space must analyze as well as *change* history.[13] The starting point of Marx's theory of history is made most vivid when he writes: "In direct contrast to German philosophy [Idealism] which descends from heaven to earth, here we ascend from earth to heaven."[14] In other words, the active life of a human as a social being is the sole ground and determination of consciousness.

In this construct, declaring that humans as social beings determine consciousness and not the other way around, Marx turns the thought of Hegel on its head. Simply, in contrast to the German tradition, Marx refuses to begin with some metaphysical

12. Marx and Engels, *The German Ideology*, 36–37.
13. See Karl Marx, *Theses on Feuerbach*, in MECW, 5:8.
14. Marx and Engels, *The German Ideology*, 36.

(most real) *a priori* concept such as God, idea, reason, intuition, consciousness, or will. Rather, he demands that we begin with the material productive forces of human life grounded in the economic structure of society. In this way, Marx secularizes the dialectical movement of Hegel's pantheistic Divine Reason into the dialectical movement of the material *Geist* (Spirit). Within this construct, Marx candidly notes that he is beginning with empirical observation and not with German idealism, but his critical evaluation does not mean he is leaving idealism completely behind. Marx's task was to synthesize idealism and empiricism in its materialistic form and, thus, to arrive at a consistent humanism that was capable of grasping the activity of the sensuous world. For this reason, Marx's theory of history begins with a human being as a praxis being in the world; history establishes the physical organization of living individuals and their relationship to the rest of nature.[15] In this, he distinguishes humans from the animal kingdom. In Marx's judgment, the first principle that distinguishes humans from animals is that the former "produce" their own means of subsistence. This production of the means of subsistence is conditioned upon the physical world surrounding humans, and, thus, Marx concludes that humans uniquely produce indirectly their own material life. This production cannot be said of the animal kingdom because brutes live by instinct and do not possess consciousness, whereas humans live by consciousness. Furthermore, human production of human means of subsistence is dependent upon the mode of production, that is, the activity or mode of life that expresses who a human being is by the reality of what is produced and how it is produced.

15. Marx states the task clearly: "The writing of history must always set out from these natural bases and their modification in the course of history through the action of men" (ibid., 31).

Productive Forces and Human Consciousness

For Marx, three primary historical relationships of production or "productive forces" initiate the historical activity of humans. His position here has much affinity with the idea of the state of nature found in secular Enlightenment thinkers, who emphasized the natural state of the human species and the requirements for survival, such as food and procreation. Marx, however, rearranges the idea of the state of nature into his own version of production. In his view of history, human activity is to be understood as "three moments" that have existed simultaneously since their beginning in the relations of production. These "three moments" are (1) the fundamental condition of humans, which presupposes their everyday needs (e.g., food, drink, clothing, shelter); (2) the production of the means that will satisfy those everyday needs (the first historical act); and (3) the reproduction of the human race, which ensures the development and interaction of the human race. In Marx's estimation, human life does not continue, nor can it be defined, unless these three aspects are present. Thus, a correct interpretation of history begins with everyday labor and human reproduction, which provide the social and natural understanding of history.

Marx's paradigm, however, is not complete; one final moment remains. Within the social relationship of humanity, a "fourth moment" is constitutive of the other three moments, namely, the "co-operation of several individuals."[16] With this fourth component, Marx recognizes that people produce what they need to satisfy their everyday necessities only when there is social interaction. Hence, essential to Marx's view of history is the relationship of "industry and exchange" (production and interaction). It does not make any difference what the conditions

16. Ibid., 43.

are, or to what end these social relationships exist. As a "mode of co-operation," the social relationship will always exist with a certain mode of production in which the mode of cooperation is a "productive force." These modes cannot be separated. Marx concludes, therefore, that the "materialistic connection of men with one another [the mode of cooperation] . . . is determined by their needs and their mode of production."[17] He also expresses this another way: "The mode of production of material life conditions the general process of social, political and intellectual life."[18] In this construct, Marx notes that fundamental to a historical interpretation of material activity is its economic structure. As we previously observed, the economic structure of society is the foundation of its superstructure. He declares that history is independent of any "political and religious nonsense" as he opens humanity to understanding consciousness within the dynamics of the interaction and integration of the four moments that constitute history. Only in the interface of these four moments do humans discover that they possess consciousness. Out of historical material arises human consciousness. As Marx puts it, "consciousness is from the very beginning a social product."[19]

Marx's conception of consciousness also incorporates an evolutionary movement that begins with brutish human characteristics: consciousness moves from its abstract to its concrete form. The consciousness of the first humans is a confrontation with the "completely alien, all-powerful and unassailable force" of nature; it is consciousness of their "*immediate* sensuous environment."[20] In this setting, consciousness of other humans is quite limited and it has little connection to things outside

17. Ibid.
18. Marx, preface to *A Contribution to the Critique of Political Economy*, 263.
19. Marx and Engels, *The German Ideology*, 44.
20. Ibid.

the immediate surroundings of the individual. Although Marx points out that the first humans were not brutes, since they lived in relationships, he speaks of those early human relationships as "purely animal consciousness of nature."[21] Interestingly, Marx calls this historical state "natural religion." In this primitive environment, Marx maintains, there was a deterministic interaction between society and the relationship of humanity to nature, but this interaction was restricted since humanity had not advanced to its socio-political stage. Marx compares people in this early stage of humanity to sheep, referring to their "herd-consciousness," or "tribal consciousness." Marx's perspective is that, even in this primordial state, consciousness operated in the context of practice; hence, development should be anticipated through the necessity of productivity, the increase of human needs, and the sustaining of these aspects through an increase in population. In this context, the division of labor emerged and would be sustained.

The Division of Labor and the Phases of Capitalism's Rise

Focusing specifically on the progressive character of Marx's theory of history, we note that within the structure of the economically productive activity of humanity there emerges a division of labor. This division of labor emerges within society when conflict arises between the relations of production and the forces of production—that is, when there is a clash between intellectual and material activity, enjoyment and labor, and production and consumption. For Marx, the division of labor that

21. Ibid. Marx's view of the initial stage of humanity had a close affinity with Jean-Jacques Rousseau's view of the initial stage. This resemblance is not a coincidence; Marx held Rousseau's treatise *What Is the Origin of Inequality among Men, and Is It Authorized by Natural Law?* (1754) in high regard.

arises is a higher state of material human existence. Further, the development of the division of labor within a given society is an expression of a new productive force in that society, such as the movement from an agrarian society to an industrial society. Thus, the different stages that arise in the division of labor are just different forms of ownership.[22] Each stage determines the relationships of individuals to each other in the context of the material, the instrument, and the product of labor. Having identified his concept of the division of labor, Marx proceeds to map out each stage in history: primitive society, Greek and Roman society, feudal ownership, and bourgeois ownership.

The first division of labor occurred when there was "tribal ownership" in primitive society.[23] At this stage, the division of labor was confined to the existing family because production was underdeveloped. Marx notes that in this primordial period two conditions became evident. First, in this social structure, there is a hierarchical gradation (chain of being), in which the patriarchal family chieftains (male heads) are at the top and members of the tribes (female adults and children) are slaves.[24] This separation occurs within the family structure itself and in the separation between the family and the rest of society. Concerning the family structure, Marx argues that the "*unequal* distribution" of work and its yield (property) occurs initially in the family itself. He is very direct, stating that the "wife and children are the slaves of the husband."[25] The husband is the first owner of property (his family), and this corresponds to the modern property-based structure of society. For Marx, the "division of labor [i.e., the

---

22. See Marx and Engels, *The German Ideology*, 32.

23. According to Robert Tucker, Marx uses the concept of the division of labor synonymously with the term *alienation*. See Robert Tucker, *Philosophy and Myth in Karl Marx*, 2nd ed. (Cambridge: Cambridge University Press, 1972), 188.

24. Marx and Engels, *The German Ideology*, 33; see also 46–47.

25. Ibid., 46.

slave labor of wife and children] and private property are, after all, identical expressions."[26]

Marx also notes that this division of labor implies that the self-interest of the individual family is in conflict with the interest of the community. The interest of the community will be connected to the material reality that surrounds it, and thus the deeds of a family, as well as the deeds of an individual, become an alien power. The reason for this alienation is that the family's or person's distribution of labor occurs in the context of the material activity of the community already in place. A deed is not an autonomous action; rather, the labor will be forced to conform (be enslaved) to the broader population in which the action has occurred.

At this point, two interesting components in Marx's thought are disclosed—his view of the truly free human and his view of a communist society. Concerning freedom, when acting for the sake of livelihood, people are not free when they conform their labor to the actions and relationships established in the community. The individual can be free, he argues, only in a communist society, in which no one is limited to one specific economic activity. In the communist society, Marx posits, a person is free to move about from one branch of production to another from day to day, or even in the same day—in the morning one can live as a hunter, in the afternoon as a fisherman, and in the evening as a cattle raiser.[27] He also posits that for this free communist society to come into existence, a key component will be that the contradictions and tensions within the division of labor will be negated—that is, the division between material and mental labor will be dissolved. He adds that the curse of being burdened by matter (nature) will be released when people live in a free, common society without the activity and stress of alienation.

26. Ibid.
27. Ibid., 47.

According to Marx, a hierarchical gradation also came into existence as humans initiated their productive forces of survival. Those who produced by means of agriculture were on the highest end of the spectrum, whereas on the lower end were those who hunted and fished. Where there was tribal and herding consciousness, the division of labor surfaced in two ways. First, it arose in the division of labor by gender, since the male, more than the female, is naturally disposed by physical strength to provide more for material needs. Second, division of labor arose in the conflict between nature (material labor) and the mental capacity to use and conquer nature (mental labor). For example, Marx remarks that the mental aspect of consciousness manages to liberate itself from the consciousness of material reality by attempting to explain the sensuous world by some transcendent concept (e.g., Plato's doctrine of Forms or the idea of a supreme being). Disciplines such as theoretical science, theology, philosophy, and ethics tend to fall into this trap. Marx reminds us that this division occurs only when social relations "have come into contradiction with existing forces of production."[28] For Marx, this same division existed in humanity's primitive environment as in the modern national consciousness or the interactions of diverse nations around the globe. Marx's ideal is for all social relationships to be in complete harmony with every object of production.

Marx refers to the second division of labor as ancient communal and state ownership (among the Greeks and Romans). This form of ownership surfaced in history as tribes united to form a city. These unions occurred either by agreement between parties or by conquest in war. Slavery continued to exist in this situation. In fact, Marx speaks of communal ownership because "citizens hold power over their laboring slaves only in

28. Ibid., 45.

their community."[29] Furthermore, Marx viewed such a community as communal *private property*; thus, only as a citizen of the community, being part of the communal ownership, can one be distinct from slaves and have power over them. In Marx's view of communal ownership, an infant stage of movable and immovable private property existed in subordinate form. This social construct eventually crumbled as the division of labor developed from immovable private property to movable private property. This transition occurred when the self-interests of those living in the towns and those living in the country become antagonistic toward each other. The towns themselves became even more disturbed when the antagonism between industry and maritime commerce developed. In other words, Marx traces within this social structure the development of a class relation between citizens and slaves—from the division of labor in communal ownership, to the self-interests of towns and countryside, to the competing claims of industry and commerce.

The third division of labor that Marx highlights is feudal or estate ownership. In contrast to the Greek and Roman communal town, the social organization of the Middle Ages emerged from the rural areas. According to Marx, this occurred because the barbarian conquest of the Roman Empire scattered the population over a large area, giving rise to a vast territory devoted to agriculture. Also, as the barbarians conquered the Roman Empire, certain productive forces declined (e.g., agriculture, industry, trade, and population). The new mode of organization determined a new mode of production. Marx describes this new mode of production as feudal property. It appeared under the weight of the "German military constitution." Marx observes that, similar to primitive tribal and communal ownership, feudal ownership was based on community. In feudal ownership,

29. Ibid., 33.

however, the producing class did not consist of slaves, but of peasants, called serfs. Feudal ownership, then, is a hierarchical structure (chain of being) of land ownership in which the serfs are found toward the bottom and the nobility is found at the top. Furthermore, the serfs produce on the land owned by the nobility.

In feudal society, according to Marx's analysis, towns existed in conflict with the country. Ownership in the towns took the form of "corporative property," by which he means "the feudal organization of trades."[30] In these municipalities, one's property was comprised mainly of the labor of one's trade, which had evolved in the setting of multiple components in a communal environment. In these towns, in hostile relationships to the landed nobility, communal markets and industrial merchants met the needs of the productive forces. Moreover, discontented serfs left the country in increasing numbers to become artisans in the towns. People in various occupations began to accumulate capital and formed a bond of corporative property known as the guild system.[31] Each craft had its own guild, which offered protection of property and increased the means of production for its members. At the same time, the guild masters organized the journeymen and apprentices (usually serfs who had escaped from their lords) according to their own personal interests. Hence, whether in the country or in the town, socioeconomic classes existed: in the country, nobility and serf, and in the town, guild master and artisan. Moreover, country and town presented contrasting divisions of labor during the feudal period. Landed property operated with "chained" serf labor, whereas town property had an individual with some capital "commanding the labor of journeymen."[32] Marx remarks that feudal society presented the

30. Ibid., 34.
31. For Marx's understanding of the rise of the guild system, see ibid., 34, 64–65.
32. Ibid., 34.

"greatest division of material and mental labor . . . [in] the separation of town and country" that history had ever witnessed.[33]

The fourth division of labor is private or bourgeoisie ownership. Before Marx maps out the three phrases of the rise of capitalism, he offers an explanation of capital during the Middle Ages. He states that capital then consisted of natural or estate capital. That is, it was associated with the specific work of the owner (e.g., house, tools of a craft, customers, vocations passed down from father to son). Within this system, however, the merchants gradually began to see opportunities to expand commerce beyond their own neighborhoods and towns. They extended trade to fellow merchants of surrounding towns, and, upon the discovery of America and the sea route to the East Indies, they expanded their markets to the world. A new division of labor emerged in this context. Marx refers to this division of labor as the separation of production and commerce, in which a special class of merchants arose.

In each town, the separation between production and commerce became solidified as new means of production emerged to provide the merchants with a competitive edge. In this context, the guild system faded as manufacturing industry began to rise, and thus the previous mode of production during the Middle Ages began to break down. Property was now "transformed into industrial or commercial capital."[34] For Marx, this transition introduced the first phase of the rise of modern capitalism. He provides the following example of this changeover in the weaving industry. In the villages and market centers, low-skilled weavers produced clothing and other products in accordance with the self-interest of manufacturers and merchants. On the backs of these weavers, these early entrepreneurs in industry and

33. Ibid., 64.
34. Ibid., 77.

the commercial market began a steady rise and accumulated wealth. The natural or estate relationship of capital between worker and employer, as in the previous guild system, became a monetary relationship between worker and employer—a relationship involving moveable capital. Because of the development of manufacturing (industry), moveable capital (money) became the form of capital in the market place. Marx calls the owners of the industrial or commercial capital the bourgeoisie (who own property), whereas those who labor for industrial or commercial capital he calls the proletariat (who do not own property). The expansion of trade and manufacturing hastened the accumulation of moveable capital and created a large bourgeoisie. In this structure of moveable and expanding capital, the proletariat became subject to the bourgeoisie.

The second phase in the rise of capitalism was characterized by commerce and navigation expanding quicker than manufacturing.[35] The goal of the nations during this period (1650–1800) was to become dominant in sea trade and colonial power. For a nation to achieve this supremacy, its manufacturing industry had to keep pace with its trade. England became the prime example of such domination in the global market. As its merchants attempted to establish their commercial monopoly, they realized that they needed state and political protection. With merchants receiving this protection, the commercial towns, especially the maritime towns, grew into large bourgeois environments. Although England became dominant in global trade and power, other European nations replicated this achievement on a lesser scale. Hence, Marx writes the following:

> This period is characterized by the cessation of the bans of the export of gold and silver and the beginning of the trade

---

35. Ibid., 70.

> in money; by banks, national debts, paper money; by spec-
> ulation in stocks and shares and stockjobbing in all articles;
> by the development of finance in general. Again capital lost
> a great part of the natural [estate] character which had still
> clung to it.[36]

Simply put, colonization in this period was solidifying the transition from estate capital (of the agrarian nobility) to commercial
capital (of the bourgeoisie). The rise of a pervasive global market
was destroying the former division of labor characteristic of the
Middle Ages, and it was establishing what would be known as
capitalism, characterized by private property—and leading to the
division between the bourgeoisie and the proletariat.

Analyzing the third phase in the rise of capitalism and private ownership, Marx turns his attention to human material
needs outgrowing the existing productive forces and, thus, the
acceleration of larger industry to meet the demand for goods. In
order to meet those needs, industry required the protection of
free competition within each industrial nation. To promote the
wealth of a nation, the state would have to protect free trade not
only within the nation but also in the global market. Big industry
now universalized competition, "established means of communication and a modern world market, subordinated trade to itself,
transformed all capital into industrial capital, and thus produced
the rapid circulation . . . and the centralization of capital."[37] In
Marx's view, this universal stage of capitalistic competition put
a strain on humanity physically, intellectually, and, most of all,
naturally. He goes so far as to state that this strain "destroyed
as far as possible ideology, religion, morality, etc., and, where

36. Ibid., 72.
37. Ibid., 73.

it could not do this, made them into a palpable lie."[38] In Marx's judgment, this stage of capitalism "produced world history for the first time."[39] By this he meant that all civilized nations and individual persons in those nations were dependent upon the new global market to satisfy their needs.

Although Marx was content with capitalism's negative effect on ideology, religion, and morality, he was displeased with its destructive effect on natural science, the natural division of labor, and the natural emergence of towns. He saw the commercial and industrial town obliterating the pleasant natural state of the countryside, of work, and of disciplines of knowledge. Marx was emphatic in stating that all natural relationships were now finding their resolution in monetary relationships. Capitalism was not only invading every realm of human life; it was the dominating force of all human life. Further, the rise of commercial and industrial capitalism was creating the same relationship between the classes in all societies it touched around the globe. This class consciousness became so pervasive that it destroyed the individual identity of a person's nationality. Marx went so far as to state that the self-interests of the bourgeoisie would deaden all nationalities. History had evolved to the point where the slave-master relationship had become the worker-capitalist relationship, and the proletariat's labor was "unbearable."

The Proletariat's State of Labor

According to Marx, the proletariat's horrendous state of labor resulted from numerous factors. First, a law of manufacturing capitalism requires that capital must increase continually and extend its domain into the global market. In Marx's judgment,

38. Ibid.
39. Ibid.

this law removed humanity from its natural state of labor. Adam Smith (1723–90) regarded dexterity to be the release of the natural talents of the individual worker, and now, Marx states, the worker has become a "crippled monstrosity," whose "capabilities and instincts" of dexterity are suppressed for the sake of productive capitalism.[40] In other words, the individual worker was bound to the demands of the capitalist in the confines of the workshop or factory. The worker's natural state of laboring independently was crushed. As far as Marx is concerned, capitalism had transformed natural, independent workers into "a productive mechanism whose parts are human beings."[41]

A second factor leading to the undesirable state of labor, in Marx's estimation, was that the mechanical power of the machine negated the muscular power of human beings, particularly that of the men in the work force. The machine was viewed as being capable of operation by any member of the family, including women and children. The capitalist was able to increase his wage-labor force by including every member of the family. Marx notes, however, that in doing so, capitalism reduced or eliminated the amount of time children had available for play as well as the amount of free labor individuals could invest in their homes. As a result, the labor power of the adult male was no longer the sole provision for the entire family. If there is a family of four, Marx says, then the labor power of four days of work done by one person is reduced to one day of work done by four people. In this case, the price of the product will fall in proportion to surplus-labor, that is, "four over the surplus-labor of one."[42] The wage-labor is no longer focused on the male head of the family; rather, it is now distributed over the family. The machine

40. Karl Marx, *Capital*, in MECW, 35:365.
41. Ibid., 343.
42. Ibid., 398.

augmented the labor force of the family and, in the process, the machine became the primary means of capital's "exploitation" of humanity's labor value.

Third, the machine increased the productivity of labor. Since the machine was now the new power of labor, the capitalist could justify expanding the work day and week of the human laborer in order to boost production. Marx assessed that such action was beyond the bounds of human nature. In the hands of the capitalist, the machine had intelligence and will that overcame the intelligence and volition of independent laborers—reducing such people to compliant and passive beings. The capitalist exploited the worker by turning the machine into a barrier between labor and human dignity. As the machine became a dominant force in industry, capitalist production and profit rose significantly, making it possible to release larger quantities of commodities at cheaper prices for the consumer. The capitalist then enhanced his profits further by extending the work day and week. How did this come about? According to Marx, the higher margin of profit only intensified the appetite of the capitalist for more gain. Once the machine became more pervasive in industry, the surplus-value of the product could increase under two circumstances: (1) The productivity from the use of labor could increase the rate of surplus-value, or (2) the number of workers could swell in order to increase productivity. When viewing the working day, the surplus-value would be determined by the surplus-labor of that day—more labor meant more value. So it seemed that an increase in the number of laborers employed would increase the amount of capital the employer made. But would the capital of the capitalist truly rise with an increase of workers? Not really. Since the machine was providing the increased power of the labor force anyway, the capitalist came to realize that capital grew more by employing the same wage earner for a longer day than by hiring multiple wage earners. To Marx, this particular way of exploiting the worker was devastating to the family unit and demonstrated that families were fully at the disposal of the capitalist. Marx puts the situation strongly, summing it up as: "that remarkable phenomenon in the history of Modern Industry, that machinery sweeps away every moral and natural restriction on the length of the working day."[43]

Fourth, changes in the division of labor resulted from the workers' use of machines. Marx identifies a number of worker classifications. There is the class of workers who operate the machine and the attendants (usually children) who assist the worker. Further classifications differentiate those who repair the machines and those who operate the machines. Marx focused his attention on the relationship between the machine and the laborer. In his perspective, capitalism had exploited and transformed the labor power of the individual who was an accomplished artisan; all that mattered now was his ability to serve a machine. "In handicrafts and manufacture, the workman makes use of a tool," Marx says, but "in the factory, the machine makes use of him."[44] Marx characterizes the capitalist's use of the machine as squeezing intellect and vitality out of the worker. The capitalist secured the power of *master* in the modern world of the industrial factory; the persons providing the labor were his *slaves*.

In Marx's assessment, this stage of capitalism almost exclusively defined England. Britain created a world market through its concentration on trade and manufactured products. She eventually came to the point where existing industrial productive forces could not meet the demands of their expanding market. Hence, new productive forces and machinery were born to meet this demand. Big industry now universalized competition,

43. Ibid., 411.
44. Ibid., 425.

"established means of communication and a modern world market, subordinated trade to itself, transformed all capital into industrial capital, and thus produced the rapid circulation . . . and the centralization of capital."[45] According to Marx, this final development of capitalism put a strain upon mankind physically, intellectually, and, most of all, naturally. It made natural science submissive to capital; the division of labor lost any aspect of natural labor that it had left. It destroyed natural growth; instead, large industrial cities emerged overnight, and the victory of the commercial town over the countryside was now complete.[46]

The modern global market set the stage for the next mode of production in history. To Marx, class struggle (the oppressor in conflict with the oppressed) is fundamental to the evolving stages of history. As we have seen, in his view, the modern era in which he lived was characterized by the struggle between the bourgeoisie and the proletariat. The increase in the means of exchange and commodities in trade, commerce, and industry, had enabled the bourgeoisie to topple the burghers from the Middle Ages and feudalism. Such a revolution could not have happened in isolation; indeed, Marx maintained that the establishment of the bourgeoisie was assisted politically by the state. In fact, "the modern State is but a committee for managing the common affairs of the whole bourgeoisie."[47] Obviously, Marx gives the bourgeoisie

45. Marx and Engels, *The German Ideology*, 73.

46. It is true that in *Capital* Marx provides a close and precise analysis of the intricacies of the system of capitalism. It should not be overlooked that his *Contribution to the Critique of Political Economy* (1859) was a serious preview of what he would expound in *Capital* (see MECW, 29–34).

47. Karl Marx and Friedrich Engels, *Manifesto of the Communist Party*, in MECW, 6:486. Concerning the difference between the feudal world and the world of capital, Marx's position has produced a formula of the relationship between commodity and money. Essentially, feudalism operates like this: C→M→C. A person sells a commodity for money, which in turn enables him to purchase other commodities. The concern in feudalism is to gain commodities that have fixed values in the market. On the

a less than favorable assessment, stating that they operate out of "naked self-interest" and "brutal exploitation." The dignity of every occupation is turned into monetary wage-labor, the family is reduced to a monetary relationship, the contentment of local and national markets becomes greed for global wealth creating a civilization in its own image, the country is dependent upon the town and city, and the forces of nature are in subjection to machinery and industry. In Marx's view, history is in position for another revolution. In fact, the bourgeoisie has created the agent of its own destruction: the proletariat. The working class exists in dependence upon employment by those with capital; they sell themselves as a commodity, "like every other article of commerce, and are consequently exposed to all the vicissitudes of competition, to all the fluctuations of the market."[48] Their labor has lost all its charm and individuality, and is merely "an appendage of the machine." Because of the dominance of the machine and its continual modernization, the workers lose their skill, their livelihood becomes more unstable, and their wages oscillate. Under these conditions, the two classes begin to clash; their antagonism will become so intense that workers will form unions against the bourgeoisie. Then riots will break out—not leading to immediate victory, but to the growth of the union movement.

As the proletarians are increasingly organized into unions, the class struggle will become a political struggle. Eventually the working class will evolve into a political party demanding legislation that addresses their working conditions. Ironically,

---

other hand, capitalism operates like this: M→C→M'. With money, a person buys a commodity, and the commodity attains a surplus-value in the sale in which the price (M' = rent, interest, and profit) fluctuates, usually to the advantage of the capitalist exploiting the worker and the customer. In capitalism, the concern is to accumulate capital (money) beyond the real value of the commodity.

48. Marx and Engels, *Manifesto of the Communist Party*, 490.

the bourgeoisie will provide the proletariat with the weapons of battle against it. The weaknesses of its own agenda will be exposed to the proletariat, and the bourgeoisie will become its own "grave digger" in the inevitable victory of the proletariat. For example, the bourgeoisie will do battle on several fronts with the aristocracy, with rival members of its own class locally and globally, and with the various antagonistic elements of industry. In order to do so, the bourgeoisie will have to appeal to the proletariat in order to secure profits, supplies, and political advantage. According to Marx, as the strain between the classes intensifies, segments of the enlightened ruling class will become sympathetic to the proletariat and join their revolutionary cause. As all these components come together, class struggle will approach its decisive hour.[49] The situation will evolve to the point where the proletariat possesses no property; the relationships within the proletariat family have no parallel to those within the bourgeois family, industrial labor and subjection to capital have stripped from the working class any national identity; and societal cornerstones such as religion, ethics, and law are dispensed with as constructs of bourgeois prejudice. In Marx's estimation, the proletariat will reach majority status in a capitalist global market, and proletarians will seize the opportunity to become masters of the productive forces of society and masters of their fate. In order to accomplish this, however, they will have to completely "destroy all previous securities for, and insurances of, individual property."[50] According to Marx, this violent overthrow of the bourgeoisie must take place within each capitalist nation as a civil war between classes, thus setting in place the conditions for communism to be established on a global scale.

49. Ibid., 494.
50. Ibid., 495.

The Dictatorship of the Proletariat

At this stage, there will still remain a step between capitalism and communism, according to Marx. The overthrow of the bourgeoisie ushers in the next necessary phase of historical materialism, often described as the dictatorship of the proletariat. Here Marx's analysis of history becomes oriented toward the future, not the past. As Marx looked forward into the unknown, he was confident that the proletariat would oust the bourgeoisie from economic and political power. Marx believed that he was living on the brink of that transition—that there would soon be the transformation of the capitalist world by revolution. The oppressive and exploitive nature of the capitalist was beginning to reach its "decisive hour." Marx had observed a number of circumstances that he thought would stimulate revolution by the proletariat, such as the organization of a political party, no possession of property, destruction of personal identity, and the annihilation of the family. But the rise of the proletariat, for Marx, was only an intermediate stage in history between capitalism and communism.[51] Marx never viewed the proletarian revolution in abstraction from its concrete goal of establishing communism; every proletarian action occurs with the consummating communist society in view. Hence, if communism is to come upon the scene of human history, then capitalism must fall. In order for this to occur, the first act of revolution by the proletariat is to gain political power and supremacy. Its dialectical tension with the bourgeoisie must evolve into establishing itself as a political party. Although the party must begin initially at the national level, in Marx's view, the proletariat eventually would organize

51. See *Letter from Karl Marx to Joseph Weydemeyer in New York*, in MECW, 39:62, 65.

politically as one organic party throughout the capitalist nations in order to accomplish its collective objectives. Why would this occur? The reason is that, as the laborers are stripped of any human dignity and become merely an extension of the capitalist machine, they really belong to no country.

When the political supremacy of the proletariat is achieved by this process, all capital will be removed from the bourgeoisie. In turn, the working class will centralize all the instruments of production and place them in the hands of the state. Immediately, the task of the proletariat will be to increase the total productive forces as quickly as possible, so that all the people will have the sufficient necessities of life. These actions must be accompanied by the abolition of the property rights of the bourgeoisie. Since the proletariat does not possess capital to own property, it must "destroy all previous securities for, and insurances of, individual property" appropriated by the capitalist.[52] Marx makes it clear that his attack is directed toward the abolition of bourgeois private property, not property in general. This point must be kept in mind when reading his declaration that the theory of communism can be summarized in one phrase: "Abolition of private property"—specifically, the abolition of bourgeois private property.[53] To attain this ultimate goal, Marx identifies the dictatorship of the proletariat as the worker's objective. He writes: "The *class rule* of the workers over the strata of the old world who are struggling against them can only last as long as the economic basis of class society has not been destroyed."[54] In other words, there can be no classless society until capitalism is dissolved. In Marx's estimation, the dictatorial activity of

---

52. Marx and Engels, *Manifesto of the Communist Party*, 495.
53. Ibid., 498.
54. Karl Marx, *Notes on Bakunin's "Statehood and Anarchy,"* in MECW, 24:521.

the proletariat is meant to produce the final stage of history—a world without classes. The implementations of the proletariat in this period, besides the turning of private property into public property, will include an income tax, the abolition of inheritance rights, the confiscation of property from emigrants and rebels, the centralization and monopoly of credit by the state's national bank, state ownership of factories and instruments of production, state centralization of communication and transportation, equal liability for all labor (industry and agriculture), the gradual elimination of the distinction between town and country, and free public education for all children.[55] Once these measures of *socialism* are in place, there will be no need for a ruling class, and any antagonism between the bourgeoisie and the proletariat will cease to exist.

The State of Communism

Marx called for an actual communist revolution, initiated by the proletariat, and her rule. The mere toppling of the bourgeoisie was never meant to be the end; rather, the destruction of the middle class was the means to an end: the state of communism. One of the strongest battle cries for revolution during the nineteenth century was voiced in *The Communist Manifesto*, which stated that communists "openly declare that their ends can be attained only by the forcible overthrow of all existing social conditions. Let the ruling classes tremble at a Communist revolution. The proletarians have nothing to lose but their chains. They have a world to win. Working men of all countries, unite!"[56] Reaching the goal of communism, in Marx's view, does

---

55. Marx and Engels, *Manifesto of the Communist Party*, 505.

56. Ibid., 519. For further insight into the Manifesto, see Terrell Carver, "The Manifesto in Marx's and Engels's Lifetimes," in *The Cambridge Companion to the Communist Manifesto*, ed. Terrell Carver and James Farr (New York: Cambridge

not mean the end of capital, labor, industry, and agriculture. Rather, human activity will be the capital of society. In this environment, human labor will be freed from the domineering dialectical and contradictory components of capitalism that brought the state of alienation between the human subject and the objectification of the means and mode of production. In communism, the powers of production, means of production, and mode of production will have surrendered to the "historic economic process" that begets a social, organic unity of all human activity without exploitation by the bourgeoisie.[57] In this organic unity, the laws of production and the laws of distribution of wealth, although distinct entities, will finally operate in equal, natural relationship to each other. The wealth of a ruling class will not exceed that of a subordinate class; in fact, the society will be classless, a circumstance brought about by the evolution of the economic conditions in history. Marx even drives home the point that communism will involve "*universal* private property" because of the annulment of private property.

Marx posits that, as history enters the stage of communism, humanity will struggle from a critical analysis of personal self-estrangement into the final, consummated state of transcendent self-estrangement. Marx expresses this transition in a number of ways. For example, as humanity enters into a state of universal property, each individual must surrender personal talent for the sake of all humanity. Marx also finds a parallel between the exploitation of workers in society and the exploitation of women in marriage. The marriage relationship, he argues, evolved into a state in which women are no longer a "*community of women*," but have become "a piece of *communal*

University Press, 2015), 67–83.

57. See Karl Marx, *A Contribution to the Critique of Political Economy*, 210. This important work preceded the publication of Marx's *Capital*.

and *common* property," especially under capitalism.[58] In other words, to use Marx's own metaphor, capitalism "prostitutes" the labor force of women for its own political and economic wealth. Simply put, the transition from the natural community of women to the exploitation of women in the marriage state illustrates the transition from humanity's natural state of labor to the exploitation of humanity under capitalism. Marx realized that this illustration would seem crude to many, yet the transitional element as it is presented in his illustration provided the term for this initial stage of communism: *crude communism.*[59] In the stage of crude communism, humanity is still overcoming such capitalistic characteristics as envy and avarice in order to abolish private property completely. Since in the global capitalistic market most of humanity (the laborer and the nonworking poor) has not attained possession of private property, the revolution must bear its fruits before envy and avarice will be negated. Once the revolution has been achieved, there will be a universal community of labor in which all receive equal wages from the communal capital, and universal peace will reign.

In support of his argument, Marx returns to what he regards as the state of nature. The communal world of communism has its foundation in the "direct, natural, and necessary" relationship between a man and a woman. Human beings are in direct and natural relationship with each other, as reflected in the "direct and procreative relationship" between the sexes.[60] For Marx, this indisputable relational activity occurs in the natural realm. In the sensuous world of nature, the essence of the human being is manifested. (For Marx, essence and existence are constitutive

---

58. Karl Marx, *Economic and Philosophic Manuscripts of 1844*, in MECW, 3:294.

59. Ibid., 295. Friedrich Engels provides further insight into the meaning of dissolving the family under communism in *The Origin of the Family, Private Property, and the State*, in MECW, 26:129–276.

60. Marx, *Economic and Philosophic Manuscripts of 1844*, 295–96.

of each other; one does not precede the other.) Only within the natural world do the male and the female in relationship as species-beings comprehend themselves as natural. Also in this context, human *need* comes into view, which points to the fact that an individual person "is at the same point a social being."[61] Only when humanity returns to its natural consciousness as a social being will the annulment of bourgeois private property come about. This return to a genuine state of social consciousness must include the annulment of the state, which is also foreign to the natural essence of the human being. Marx notes that, in the condition of crude communism, complete release from the chains of private property will accompany the departure of the last remnants of the state. So, as communism frees humanity from its self-estrangement (self-alienation) by transcending the current factors of estrangement, history will move into its fully consummated state.

In summarizing his conception of history, Marx remarks: "The entire movement of history, just as its [communism's] *actual* act of genesis—the birth act of its empirical existence—is, therefore, also for its thinking consciousness the *comprehended* and *known* process of its *becoming*."[62] Communism is, thus, the final state of history. Marx makes this point clear:

> This communism, as fully developed naturalism equals humanism, and as fully developed humanism equals naturalism; it is the *genuine* resolution of the conflict between man and nature and between man and man—the true resolution of the strife between existence and essence, between objectification and self-confirmation, between freedom and necessity, between the individual and the species.

61. Ibid., 298.
62. Ibid., 297.

Communism is the riddle of history solved, and it knows itself to be this solution.[63]

Since, for Marx, communism and natural societal self-consciousness are equivalent, he argues as if history possesses its own self-consciousness of resolution, redemption, and consummation (destiny), brought about by the forces, means, and modes of production that have transgressed natural humanism. Hence, communism will be the full transformation of all cultural, socio-political, economic entities. With this being said, the *cornerstone* of liberating the populace from this state of alienation will be the economic estrangement from capitalism, an estrangement in which consciousness and real life are integrated into natural social life and action, as recovered in the transcendent realm of communism. Furthermore, to Marx, religion is created by humanity's inner life to deal with the exploitation of their natural state as the various modes of production emerge in history. For this reason, Marx states that communism begins with atheism; indeed, he mentions religion first in the list of the artifacts of culture above, because for him the "criticism of religion is the premise of all criticism."[64]

In humanity's unwillingness to address its self-consciousness in the natural state of society, people create religion in order to find reality in heaven and in a supernatural being. In Marx's judgment, religion has shown itself throughout history to be an *"inverted world consciousness."* In other words, humans have made this world of fantasy and illusion their real world from which all human existence is perceived. According to Marx, humans face a dialectical tension here. They face struggle and suffering

63. Ibid., 296–97.
64. Marx, *Contribution to the Critique of Hegel's Philosophy of Law: Introduction*, 175.

for the religion they endorse, and, at the same time, their original, natural state protests against the struggle and suffering of the religion they have created. Within this context, Marx writes: "Religion is the sigh of the oppressed creature, the sentiment of a heartless world, and the soul of soulless conditions. It is the *opium* of the people."[65] Religion, through the metaphor of opium, exploits humans and results in heartless and soulless persons. Furthermore, religion is used throughout history by the capitalist ruling class to drive the masses into submission. Hence, communism begins with the abolition of religion, so that the plague of illusory happiness can be turned into real happiness. The criticism of religion is to provide a chain reaction, so that the true, secular form of societal happiness can be experienced in the full life of communism. Marx explains the domino effect in this manner: "The criticism of heaven is transformed into the criticism of earth, the *criticism of religion* into the *criticism of law*, and the *criticism of theology* into the *criticism of politics*."[66] Marx believed that the heavenly nature of religion alienated people from their natural state of life, that religion brought in a canon of unnatural law that rules over humanity instead of establishing natural law as the basis of jurisprudence.

So, how is the "riddle of history" solved through the eyes of Karl Marx? The riddle of history is solved only through a fully developed naturalism and humanism coming to life in the material activity of history. Marx calls this "communism." In this eschatological realm of material activity, private property will be abolished, labor in town and country will no longer be isolated and divided, and, thus, the separation between mental

65. Ibid. This famous quote has been attributed to various people; it has been claimed that Marx received it from Bruno Bauer. The quote is also accredited to Marquis de Sade (1740–1814), as well as to Novalis (1772–1801).

66. Marx, *Contribution to the Critique of Hegel's Philosophy of Law: Introduction*, 175.

and material activity will cease. The communist revolution of material life, or the revolution of the working class (proletariat), will seize the means of production in order to change the mode of production.[67] The mode of production will become the common, natural activity of universal humanity. Finally, humanity will be free.

67. As Marx writes: "The proletarians cannot become masters of the productive forces of society, except by abolishing their own previous mode of appropriation, and thereby also every other previous mode of appropriation. They have nothing of their own to secure and to fortify; their mission is to destroy all previous securities for, and insurances of, individual property" (Marx and Engels, *Manifesto of the Communist Party*, 495).

4

A PRESUPPOSITIONAL CRITIQUE OF MARX'S VIEW OF HISTORY

God's Plan versus Marx's Plan

Paul Johnson opens his discussion of Marx with this captivating remark: "Karl Marx has had more impact on actual events, as well as on the minds of men and women, than any other intellectual in modern times."[1] Besides the various political and military revolutions throughout the twentieth century that invoked his name, a certain mind-set has engulfed humanity, a mind-set for which his name serves as a powerful backdrop. Louis Dumont makes the point well when he notes that for the person "in the street the predominance of economic phenomena in social life is one, perhaps the first, article of [Marx's] creed."[2] In fact, this

---

1. Paul Johnson, *Intellectuals* (New York: Harper Perennial, 1988), 52.
2. Louis Dumont, *From Mandeville to Marx: The Genesis and Triumph of Economic Ideology* (Chicago: University of Chicago Press, 1977), 111.

creed has become so pervasive that Marx's view of economic parity has become the judge and jury of politico-social justice in the capitalist world. Even a capitalist who rejects Marx's position cannot avoid the call for a wider distribution of wealth as an essential aspect of cultural consciousness. After capitalism's displacement of feudalism and mercantilism, the concept of equality has been increasingly defined in a democratic society with an economic focus—whether the discussion includes redistributing wealth or simply increasing the standard of living for the poor.

Marx's view of the coming better day of economic justice looks beyond the scope of the isolated individual; indeed, it expands into a panoramic view of humanity as a "species-being" moving to a just end of commonwealth, equality, liberty, fraternity, and unity. Clearly, like many views of history in the nineteenth century, Marx's perspective is eschatological. A close examination of his position would easily uncover his view that the *end* of history (communism) defines the *beginning* of history (natural, primordial existence); the end determines the beginning. In Hegelian fashion, the end is the *concrete* consummation of the *abstract* beginning. Furthermore, to unfold Marx's view of eschatological history means to unfold his system of salvation for humanity. These two points must be stressed in our critical analysis, as they direct us to the fundamental core of secularization in Marx's philosophy of history.

In the Reformed Christian tradition, Geerhardus Vos and Cornelius Van Til both stressed that biblical revelation is eminently eschatological in character—that the end determines the beginning, and that to unfold the eschatological fabric of revelation is to unfold God's view of salvation for humanity. A comparison of the teleological, eschatological structure of biblical revelation and of Marx's thought lays bare their antithetical content, and Marx's secular humanism is revealed.

Marx and Engels place this antithesis before us like this: "*Real humanism* has no more dangerous enemy in Germany than *spiritualism* or *speculative idealism*, which substitutes '*self*-consciousness' or the '*spirit*' for the *real individual man* and with the evangelist teaches: 'It is the spirit that quickeneth; the flesh profiteth nothing.' Needless to say, this incorporeal spirit is spiritual only in its imagination."[3] Clearly included by Marx and Engels as a component of spiritualism in Germany is orthodox Christianity, which they view as a treacherous enemy to humanism. As Owen Chadwick has noted, "The theory of Marxism lies near the heart of the European problem of the secular."[4]

Without a doubt, the Christian who is confronting Marx's secular and humanistic philosophy of history must be armed with the authority of Christ, testifying to the triune God's revelatory activity throughout history as recorded in Scripture. The centrality and authority of Christ can never be separated from the facts of history. Furthermore, the facts of history cannot be truly known, interpreted, and understood outside the framework of Christ's authority. For this reason, Christ's testimony to the facts must always be comprehended within the framework of the one unified *plan* of God for the world as revealed in Scripture. Simply put, every fact is a revelational fact, controlled and exposed by the counsel of God's sovereign will. In God's sovereign plan, after the *state of innocence* in which God placed the first man and woman, the *state of sin* resulted because of the willing act of rebellion by the first man and woman. Despite their revolt, God came to them and placed them in a *state of grace* by means of his forgiving love.

---

3. Friedrich Engels and Karl Marx, forward to *The Holy Family, or Critique of Critical Criticism: Against Bruno Bauer and Company*," in MECW, 4:7.

4. Owen Chadwick, *The Secularization of the European Mind in the Nineteenth*

Because of the entrance of sin and God's grace, humanity was divided into two worlds—those who are redeemed from sin by grace in the promise and coming of Christ, and those who continually live as an expression of their fallen nature in union with the deceit and immorality of the Evil One. Christ's written revelation presents these two worlds as being antithetical to each other. The two kingdoms in conflict in his Word are known as the seed of the woman (Eve) and the seed of the serpent (Satan), the kingdom of God and the kingdom of Satan, and the age to come and the present evil age (Gen. 3:15; Mark 1:15; Eph. 1:21; Gal. 1:4). Augustine (354–430), in his discourse on a biblical philosophy of history, referred to this biblical paradigm as two cities: the city of God and the city of man. For the person in Christ's kingdom, the method and interpretation of facts must be based completely upon the eschatological, redemptive, and covenantal story in the Bible. For the person in Satan's kingdom, the method and interpretation of facts will be based completely upon chance and randomness under deterministic laws.[5] Interestingly, a critical analysis of Marx's philosophy of history falls easily into this biblical paradigm. Rejecting the religion of the Bible, he regarded the universe as having come into existence by chance and randomness and as subject to certain natural laws that fit his presuppositions of nature and human life.

In line with the critical thought of the Enlightenment, Marx concluded that the criticism of religion had come to its apex in Germany, which had finally freed humanity from a supernatural being, the fantasy of heaven, illusionary happiness, the exaltation of suffering for one's faith, and moral compliance with

---

Century (Cambridge: Cambridge University Press, 1975), 48.

5. See Cornelius Van Til, *The Doctrine of Scripture* (Phillipsburg, NJ: Presbyterian and Reformed, 1967), 5.

the rules of a supreme being. Regarding religion as an illusion, Marx states that "the *task of history*, therefore, once the *world beyond the truth* has disappeared, is to establish the *truth of this world*."[6] Once religion —notably Christianity and Judaism— disappeared from the world, in Marx's view, natural societal consciousness would recover and be in position to make its impact upon humanity.

However, a critical examination of Marx exposes his thought to be the product of the seed of the serpent and the present evil age. In order to attack the present state and the historical roots of civilization, Marx assaulted the religious nature of the human being as image of God. He, like all human beings, understood that religion was at the heart of human existence (Rom. 1:19). In his rebellion against the God of the Bible, he had to release the heart from religion in order to justify the revival of natural humanism in his era. In other words, Marx had to presuppose the truth of biblical religion—that is, the veracity of God's providential activity in history from creation to consummation—in order to reject or attack that sacred religion. Specifically, all the facts that Marx was examining exist as they are because God has created and sustained them that way. Because of God's person and activity, everything occurs and appears to be as it is. Marx took God's created and sustained facts and perverted their origin and meaning. He was a thief: he stole the truth of God's created reality and turned it into a lie, serving the mythological construct of the creature, rather than the truth of the Creator (Rom. 1:25). Hence, Marx demonstrated the biblical truth that humans are created in the image of God (Rom. 1:19), in order to discard the reality that humans are the image of God.

---

6. Karl Marx, *Contribution to the Critique of Hegel's Philosophy of Law: Introduction,* in MECW, 3:176.

The Fourfold State of
Humanity Confronts Marx

The State of Innocence

On the heels of the Enlightenment and Romanticism, Marx exchanged the religion of the Bible for his own secular religion of the heart—a religion of critical, rational empiricism that advocates a natural societal humanism. In the Protestant tradition, the Westminster Confession of Faith (WCF) provides a wonderful paradigm of the history of biblical revelation by which to analyze Marx's philosophy of materialistic and humanistic history; it is called the fourfold state of humanity (chapter 9). Almost every system of thought has a viewpoint that encompasses a fourfold pattern of existence: an explanation of the origin of things, an explanation for disorder and/or evil in the world, the resolution to the problem of disorder and/or evil, and a future hope of tranquility in contrast to the previous state. The WCF's biblical paradigm begins with the first state, called innocence. For Marx, the state of innocence is merely the original humans living to sustain their existence in natural surroundings. These humans were not much more advanced than the brutes, or animal world. In fact, sounding like Rousseau, Marx refers to the primitive state of humanity as "herd-consciousness," stressing the point that humans began with concrete living activity (praxis) in the real, material world. For Marx, human life determines consciousness. The natural world provides the material for survival as people produce (industry and exchange) the sustaining means necessary for that survival. The activity of procreation also ensures survival, testifying to the immediate interaction and development of humans. Marx began with the productive forces of human life—what he called societal consciousness—grounded in the economic structure of society. At this point, we are peering into the heart of Marx's whole system of thought—his Archimedean point, that is, that economic activity is the foundation of the superstructure of societal consciousness.[7] Specifically, the forces of production, the division of labor, and the mode as well as the means of production are among the essential characteristics of human life. Upon this foundation, Marx declared his commitment to, and faith in, natural humanism.

Since the God of the Bible is the actual creator of all natural phenomena, and since all the facts seen and interpreted are God's facts, Marx must presuppose the activity of God's creating all things in order to pervert God's beautiful creation into his own construct of the sensuous world. The praxis of God in relation to nature is completely antithetical to Marx's human praxis as creator of the material world. In this we see that interpreting one fact outside the framework of the plan and purpose of God makes all resulting facts lack coherency. Marx has reduced human essence, in the state of innocence, to an economic societal being. The full-orbed image of God is destroyed in his construction. John Calvin's position that a correct understanding of God is necessary for a correct understanding of man, and a correct understanding of man in God's image is necessary for a correct understanding of God, is completely suppressed in Marx's construct. Marx's position can only produce one result: a world of societal consciousness dominated by natural conflict and alienation throughout history, radiating from its epicenter—economics. Essentially, this consciousness has been the by-product of those who have aligned themselves with Marx and Marxist thought.

---

7. Many scholars have suggested that economics is the Archimedean point—the transcendental heart or center of Marx's system of thought. I agree. Granted, it is economics shaped by his empirical rationalism. I am aware of the debate on this issue—e.g., the suggestion of the forces of production and the challenging argument for praxis by Richard J. Bernstein (see his *Praxis and Action* [Philadelphia: University of Pennsylvania Press, 1971], 13).

For Marx, human consciousness is a social entity, connecting the individual to other persons (I-thou) and to nature (I-it). The "herd-consciousness" (I-thou) operates as a group's conscious instinct. This instinct is viewed through the lens of economic interaction; specifically, the forces of production equal the "herd-consciousness," the development and extension of human needs contextualize the means and mode of production, and the act of procreation is the first act of the division of labor. Marx affirmed the essence of man as a freely acting species-being while, at the same time, he acknowledged that the estrangement of labor degrades the free activity of human life. Prior to the ontological discussions in the twentieth century, Marx seemed to be constructing his own version of pure being to be the essential being of free activity as a species-being. For Marx, humans in this state, unlike the brutes, make their life activity the object of their will and of their consciousness.[8] Furthermore, this free life activity is related to what he refers to as the "sphere of inorganic nature." In fact, Marx notes that in this state "nature is man's *inorganic body*—nature, that is, insofar as it is not itself the human body."[9] In maintaining that a person lives on nature, his point is that "nature is his *body*, with which he must remain in continuous intercourse if he is not to die."[10]

In terms of the free activity of man, Marx held that by means of his personal activity, man creates a world of objects, which proves himself to be a conscious species-being. Marx calls this activity man's "*work upon* inorganic nature."[11] For Marx, this free activity of labor in the objective world demonstrated the advancement of humans beyond the brutes. For example, brutes only produce in the context of immediate physical

8. Karl Marx, *Economic and Philosophic Manuscripts of 1844*, in MECW, 3:277.
9. Ibid., 275.
10. Ibid., 276.
11. Ibid.

need, whereas humans produce freely for physical need, but are also free to produce outside the bounds of physical need (the dialectical tension of the original state of the human will). Furthermore, brutes produce only for themselves, for their own bodies in accordance with the natural laws of their species. On the other hand, humans produce the whole of nature in free confrontation with their product, since humans possess the intelligence to understand the natural laws of every species and also to understand how to apply those laws to the object.[12] In this free activity, labor functions as the *"objectification of man's species life."*[13] In Marx's view, contrary to the biblical text in Genesis 1–2, humans actively create the real world with the natural material that has spontaneously come into existence by its own process. The essence and existence of human activity is co-constitutive of conscious species-being—it is the pure natural state of conscious, autonomous life.

Marx's position on the original, natural state of human beings is built upon a *speculative* construct of human reason. Marx is limited to his own human ability to envision that original state; his mind does not have the capacity to provide an authoritative construct of that primitive condition. Of course, other finite minds have offered alternative understandings of the original state of human beings (e.g., Thomas Hobbes, John Locke, Jean-Jacques Rousseau, Adam Smith). Like others, Marx is dependent upon his own presuppositions as he combines the projections of his own autonomous use of reason, intuition, and imagination with his experience of the natural world. Moreover, Marx has no explanation of the innate entity that constitutes human instinct or consciousness that can explain why human beings develop or exist in a different state than the brutes. After rejecting the

12. See ibid., 277.
13. Ibid.

authority of God's interpretation of the original, natural state of human existence (innocence), Marx, like his secular comrades, is stuck in a mythological view of the beginning of history—a view that is not supported by any concrete, authoritative evidence that can truly challenge the truth that God has revealed.

The State of Sin

Upon a close examination of Marx's construct, the question arises whether such a state of free life activity actually ever existed. Marx's position is that, in dialectical tension, human activity is immediately confronted with estranged labor, in relationship both with nature and with the self. This leads to Marx's conception of the state of sin (humanity's fall from innocence). As soon as the product of labor is created as an external object, the activity of labor becomes alienated (estranged) from the human because the person enters into a new and different relationship with the object. First, the object becomes an alien object, exercising power over the person. In this condition, labor is no longer a free, internal, spontaneous act to satisfy a need; rather, labor becomes a forced action to satisfy needs external to it.[14] Marx held that, when the product of someone's creative activity thus belongs to another, one's self is lost. Marx saw this as the alienation of the *thing* (an object created from the material of nature). Second, there is the alienation of the *self* (self-estrangement). As the object is created, it becomes viewed as an independent object, seeming to have a life of its own, without the worker's own physical and mental capacities being necessary any longer. The self is alienated from viewing the object as dependent upon, and belonging to, the self. In this manner, the species-being is transformed into an abstract and isolated individual. To Marx, this transformation specifically

14. Ibid., 274.

occurs when the spontaneous, free activity of labor turns into a *means* to physical existence. According to Marx, this action is contrary to the natural essence of the human being, alienating nature as the person's inorganic body. In this state, the human's own body is estranged from the self.

Marx provides a helpful distinction for viewing this dialectical tension. As long as human labor freely creates an object in the immediate sense to satisfy physical need, the human remains within the unity of the essence of societal species-being. But once human labor creates an object for the physical subsistence of one's own economic use, the person becomes a slave in bondage to the object, placing the laborer in an antagonistic relationship with nature and self (the human's fall from innocence). One should not overlook that in Marx's natural and materialistic view of history, sin is redefined as a subject-object relationship of tension in the domain of freedom, nature, and self, with a particular focus on the alienating effects of labor in an economic life. Humanity's fall from the state of innocence has nothing to do with alienation from a personal relationship with the Creator. Indeed, God's Word tells us that, because of the fall, the ground is cursed for the sake of humanity, as people labor with sweat (Gen. 3:17–19). How can this judgment upon humanity be for humanity's sake? The curse and sweat serve to drive people to Christ. God provides relief from the curse brought about by humanity's senseless act of rebellion against the Creator. This relief is seen in one of the great invitation texts in Scripture: "Come to Me, all you who labor and are heavy laden, and I will give you rest" (Matt. 11:28). It is a rest that involves believers being joint heirs with Christ over the creation (Rom. 8:12–25). Marx viewed this as mythology and replaced it with his view of the fallen world. Instead, he should have demythologized his own imagined world in order to truly hear the good intention of the call of the gospel from the Lord of the cosmos. The stress and alienation of labor can only be resolved in the person and work of Christ, who alone returns fallen humanity to the goodness of labor expressed and celebrated in the speech of God—a glorious new creation even exceeding the original.

For Marx, the human activity of estranged labor not only affects people's relationship with nature and the self, but also brings alienation between humans. Instead of creating an object as a free, conscious species-being—one who has a corporate and unified natural societal consciousness (I-thou)—the creation of the object becomes a means of existence for the self that alienates the worker from others. The object becomes a source of competition as a means of existence between humans. Implicit in this construct for Marx is that this dynamic places the human laborer in the context of a political economy. The political aspect arises as a constitutive component of estranged labor in order to protect the means of self-existence (economically conceived) of one human against another. Even so, Marx raises an interesting issue at this point: "If the product of labor is alien to me, if it confronts me as an alien power, to whom, then, does it belong?" Marx's response is that it must belong "to a being *other* than myself."[15] Marx contends that, in past primitive and ancient cultures, the other being to whom the object belonged was the gods. In the modern era, however, such primitive deities have become extinct. In this epoch, the production and benefit of labor can only be directed to people. Then, since the object of the laborer is alien to the self, the human relationship "for a being other than myself" in a political economy will be enjoyment to one person (the profiteer), but agony to the laborer.

For Marx, the state of the fall is the state of alienation. In contrast to what God's Word says, the presupposition of Marx's

15. Ibid., 278.

end of history (communism) shapes his own version of the dilemma facing humanity. As we have seen, a dialectical tension between the self and labor confronted people almost as soon as as humanity appeared upon the scene. Because of this almost immediate tension, it is difficult to distinguish between the state of innocence and the state of the fall in Marx's thought. Marx converted the original trial of humanity into the temptation of labor for the human self. Alienation occurs if the self exceeds the free use of nature for the necessities of self-preservation. Once labor is used for economic reasons, it brings alienation (fall) from nature, self, and other human beings. In this way, Marx is manufacturing an economic foundation for human existence in which the relationship between humans themselves and the objects that humans produce turns into class warfare. Again, on the basis of his empirical method of interpreting history, Marx provides no authoritative evidence for this particular and limited construct of economic alienation as central to human alienation from nature, self, and others. Even so, in Marx's construct of the modern global economy, the worker needs redemption—redemption, that is, from the oppressive profiteer—the capitalist.

The State of Grace

Returning once again to the biblical paradigm outlined in the Westminster Standards, the state of grace, as applied to Marx's position, involves revolution changing the world and leading it toward its final state. It is a proletarian rebellion that inaugurates the transition into politico-economic socialism. The concern here for Marx is not that there is a transfer of power from the bourgeoisie to the proletariat, so that the latter becomes the new oppressor of humanity; rather, the proletariat has the task of implementing the conditions that will overcome alienation and estrangement for the human species in relationship with nature, the self, and others. Human activity and labor must move to recover the original intent of natural essence and existence. The dictatorship of the proletariat is the means to that end, with the autocracy serving as a means of mercy and grace that confronts the injustice of bourgeois exploitation. Redemption from the oppression of the bourgeoisie is liberation. Specifically, the proletariat, who are without property, must become the masters of the productive forces by abolishing "all previous securities for, and insurances of, individual property."[16] In order to achieve this goal, the proletariat will implement a system of democratic socialism through the power of the state to move toward a classless society. All the instruments of production will have to be centralized in the state in order to destroy all the economic bases for class warfare. State socialism becomes the instrumental means of redemption, moving toward the triumph of communism. Workers must put their confidence and faith in their own human activity to achieve deliverance from their oppressors. The worker alone, by his own activity (works righteousness) of revolt, is called to achieve this transformation of societal life. All laws put in place by the state to achieve the means and cause of redemption will be legalistic. The meritorious exhibition of redemption will be on display and tyrannically enforced, despite Marx's claim to the contrary. Like all non-Christian systems of thought, Marx's view of redemption exchanges the truth of God's grace for the fraud of human achievement. It requires an active life of vanity, self-righteousness, and self-serving human law to accomplish its purpose.

Again, Marx must presuppose the truth of the Christian world in order not only to attack Christianity, but also to develop his own construction of fallen humanity and redemption. Whenever

---

16. Karl Marx and Friedrich Engels, *Manifesto of the Communist Party*, in MECW, 6:495.

the non-Christian is at war with the living God, that unbeliever will create a world from within the existing cultural context. It was no different for Marx. He savored the Enlightenment's confrontation with the *ancien régime* as well as the evolution of German idealism from Kant to Hegel and the Young Hegelians. Yet, in this world of critical analysis, he found little sympathy for the task of creating a system of thought that would be truly practical, transforming the dialectical tension in the world.[17] For Marx, democratic capitalism rose to the forefront of the practical world around him. His eyes focused on the liberating effects of democratic principles applied to the politico-economic sphere of life. Indeed, to Marx, economics was the center of human essence and existence. So, since he is created in the image of God and is a human being in union with Adam's sin, it should not be surprising that he would theorize a state of sin (economic injustice) that would line up with the original innocent state (a state of natural economic justice for all). Furthermore, as one who knows he needs grace and redemption from the God of the Bible, he would create a new world of grace and redemption that would secure economic justice, embodied in the liberation of the proletariat—the workers—as the vehicle of grace, from the oppressive and exploitive yoke of the bourgeois capitalist. Like all systems created from a non-Christian perspective, Marx's system is created in the image of his own human obsession and, since it is a conception that comes from a darkened heart, its goal can only be achieved by human activity (grace is dissolved by human works). To be sure, it will always fail to achieve its goal because all human activity to redeem itself crumbles. Since the tower of Babel, all the various imaginations of humanity that are in contention against the true God have been placed by God in battle against each other. Furthermore, any non-Christian

17. See Karl Marx, *Theses on Feuerbach*, in MECW, 5:6–8.

system that proclaims salvation from self-perceived wrongs must advocate some type of revolution or transformation to achieve it, followed by some form of tyranny to secure its continuance. Laws must then be constructed in accordance with the system's view of saving grace, and these laws will always be based upon works in conformity to the humanly constructed socio-political civilization put in place.

If such a civilization tyrannically takes its position in history, claiming the prospect of an eventually unified global society, the evidence of God's activity at Babel will emerge to challenge and confound it. In the biblical conception of fallen humanity, there will always be a self-proclaimed redeemer who challenges the status quo of the socio-political state. No matter how optimistic Marx was regarding his materialistic, dialectical scheme, he possessed no evidence from history that his fabrication would prove to be the socioeconomic resolution of human alienation. In fact, a full understanding of the effects of the fall in history point to the impossibility of such redemption. After all, Marx's construction of resolution was to crumble before his own eyes. As we have already pointed out, Marx was caught in a power struggle among fellow communists in his lifetime, and such struggles have continued among communists ever since his death. Indeed, greed for power will never pass from the scene of human governments, political parties, and systems of socio-political thought, including the Marxian tradition.

As we have reflected upon the contrasting perceptions of innocence, fall, and redemption in Christian biblical revelation and in Marx, it should be clear that to unpack the structures and Archimedean point of Marx's view of history, one needs to grasp that Marx's directive is a product of various influences from his era. He endorsed Enlightenment critical thought by placing the history of religion and Christian theism on trial using the vehicle of finite empirical reason. Although he found kinship with the ancient formulation of Epicurean empirical materialism, he updated that materialism with a modern, naturalistic view of history, notably mapped out in Rousseau's *Origin of Inequality*. Additionally, it is not surprising that Marx was extremely fond of Darwin's *Origins of Species* (1859), seeing in it scientific credence for the basic tenets he adopted from Rousseau's view of history. Meanwhile, he secularized Hegel's pantheistic dialectical paradigm into a dialectical historical movement of material societal consciousness in which class conflict will eventually cease. As Marx became persuaded that the centerpiece of this secular, materialistic world is economics, he identified the accumulation and distribution of capital as the prism through which to view the varieties of human experience and activity. As far as he could see, capitalism was the source of class warfare, since it meant the exploitation and oppression of the masses by greedy, self-interested profiteers. His system of thought presupposed this role for capitalism in constructing his dialectical theory of history. The redemptive revolution of the proletariat, therefore, becomes necessary.

At this point, it may be well to note an insight from Marx that has long struck the present author positively, namely, Marx's psychological analysis of avarice and greed on the part of the capitalist. Marx would deny that his analysis presupposes the truth of biblical revelation; nevertheless, while attempting to remain within naturalistic humanism, he takes his readers into the psychology of avarice and greed, not contradicting the biblical view of this particular sin. In the Reformed Christian tradition, this insight in Marx would be attributed to common grace. Marx clearly understood capitalism's transition in the political economy during the Enlightenment—that is, its turning of the traditional Western vices of self-interest, passions, and greed into virtues. Marx rejects this stance; in fact, he views these human characteristics as vices. He goes even deeper: he maintains that human passions belong to the natural construct of humanity's essential being. In this context, objects fall under the domain of sensual gratification, not only as objects of simple reflection, but also as objects for practical activity.[18] Marx's analysis of property and money should make any Christian defender of, or sympathizer with, capitalism, take notice:

> By possessing the *property* of buying everything, by possessing the property of appropriating all objects, *money* is thus the *object* of eminent possession. The universality of its *property* is the omnipotence of its being. It is therefore regarded as omnipotent. . . . Money is the *procurer* [pimp] between man's need and the object, between his life and his means of life. But *that which* mediates *my* life for me, also *mediates* the existence of other people for *me*. For me it is the *other* person.[19]

As Marx applies God's attributes to property and money (using the words *omnipotence, almighty,* and *mediates*), he invokes the analysis of Goethe and Shakespeare to become even more pointed:

> The extent of the power of money is the extent of my power. Money's properties are my—the possessor's—properties and essential powers. Thus, what *I am* and *am capable* of is by no means determined by my individuality. I *am* ugly, but I can buy for myself the most *beautiful* of women. Therefore I am not *ugly,* for the effect of *ugliness*—its deterrent power—is nullified by money. I, according to my individual characteristics, am lame, but money furnishes me with twenty-four feet.

18. Marx, *Economic and Philosophic Manuscripts of 1844,* 322.
19. Ibid., 323.

> Therefore I am not lame. I am bad, dishonest, unscrupulous, stupid: but money is honored, and hence good.[20]

Marx clearly exposes the practical consciousness of money in the context of the emerging capitalistic global political economy. Only the Christian willfully blind to the seduction of human passions in the realm of money, power, greed, and avarice will fail to see their connection with human vices. Even so, Marx's position has an internal problem.

This ontological affirmation of vices in the original state of humanity produces a tension with Marx's other position that humans seem to be free from those vices if they interact only with the natural world to produce their essential needs—humanity's true original state of innocence. In order to resolve this tension, Marx would probably say that these vices are part of humanity's ontological nature because humans also had the ability to produce freely only within the bounds of physical need. Then, since Marx maintains that the passions are essential to the *ontological nature* of the human species in which objects are set before humans as gratification to their sensuous practical activity, Marx's redeeming sedative of political socialism and communism will never resolve such an essential conflict between these components of the nature of humanity. To place confidence in the human will to return to a state that bypasses the sensual gratification of wealth and power is sheer illusion. Moreover, the Christian needs to note that Marx's ontological understanding of the essence of human nature does not correspond to the biblical state of ontological innocence as the WCF interprets the creation narrative in Genesis. Marx provides helpful psychological insight regarding a person's sinful perception and use of capital and money, but, according to

---

20. Ibid., 324.

the Scriptures, this was not the condition of the created state of Adam and Eve in original righteousness. Adam's original sin was not an offense toward the objectification of nature; rather, his sin was against the authority and knowledge of his personal Creator. Again, Marx's view of the capitalistic roots in the essential nature of humanity is limited to his own observations and the presuppositions of the political economy in his own day. He offers no authority and no evidence beyond his own imaginative thoughts and, thus, his common-grace insights are antithetical to the authority and evidence of the biblical text.[21]

The State of Glory

Who, then, is the true child of the holy trinity of the Enlightenment—liberty, equality, and fraternity? Is it capitalism or is it communism? For Marx, the nineteenth-century battle between these two had at stake the preservation of human history. Like a romantic, his imagination created, molded, and shaped every aspect of history, from its beginning to its end, around the final triumph of communism. His vision of the end, a communist paradise, determined the beginning. His narrative is a mythology that satisfies the obsession of his own psyche to suppress the truth of God in unrighteousness. Only in this story line of saving humanity will his goals for freedom, egalitarianism, and brotherhood be realized. In communism, Marx saw mankind as able to become what they ought to be as a species-being, freely acting in nature (as one's inorganic body), no longer alienated from nature, self, and others.

Considering what the Westminster Standards note as the fourth state of humanity, we should keep in mind that Marx

---

21. For an example of how to apply antithesis and common grace as a method of Christian critique, see William D. Dennison, "Antithesis, Common Grace, and Plato's View of the Soul," in *In Defense of the Eschaton: Essays in Reformed Apologetics*, ed. James Douglas Baird (Eugene, OR: Wipf & Stock, 2015), 55–80.

was not a secular nihilist; rather, he provided hope to the world through his system. His state of glory, or system of hope, is communism. The goal of the dictatorship of the proletariat is to initiate the era of redemption through state-controlled democratic socialism. In this, the state implements economic policies that will eventually dissolve any and all economic advantages of self-interest for the bourgeoisie by abolishing private property and rights of inheritance, centralizing credit by a national bank, centralizing communication and transportation, state ownership of the instruments of production, equal liability of all labor, and free education.[22] For Marx, these policies must be implemented in order to eliminate the conditions and the expression of estrangement and alienation at the heart of human fallenness.

Indeed, Marx declared that he was creating heaven on earth. He was out to construct an earthly religion that transformed the traditional Christian understanding of heavenly glory into a humanly created material paradise of true equality and economic justice. This is a heaven consummated by human works. After all, for Marx, history is determined by the forces of economic class warfare. Specifically, in Marx's state of glory, such equality and justice are achieved by communism. In contrast, for Christianity, the final consummation of heavenly existence arrives solely by grace; God ushers in the final state of glory. God's supreme gift of grace is not based on economic justice; rather, it is based upon his own justice for sinners through his Son, justice that reconciles sinners to the triune God of the Bible and invites them to enter into the eternal worship of the Lamb of God (Rev. 5:1–14).

In Marx's estimation, the consummated state of communism returns humanity to its original condition of natural, materialistic humanism in which humans, as conscious species-beings, act freely without the division of labor. The advancement of cultural

---

22. See Marx and Engels, *Manifesto of the Communist Party*, 505–6.

artifacts, such as the products of industry, will be present. The ingenuity of human creativity, the forces of production, will be free, however, from alienation and estrangement. In Marx's heaven on earth, all the impediments to internal and external peaceful coexistence among all humans are removed. The unity of the human race is visible in such manifestations as the abolition of class, private property, the state, the family, the distinction between towns and country, and capitalistic wage-labor. The essence and existence of human nature are returned to their original constitutive state, in which the economic heart of human lives is the freedom of equal and fraternal justice. However, one of the finest secular critiques of Marx's concept of this freedom arrived in the twentieth century, when, while confessing human alienation from God, Sartre cries out that the modern human is "condemned to be free."[23] Human freedom brings condemnation upon the self. Freedom is nothing but bondage to alienation within the self. A human system declaring freedom from oppression becomes, through its own model of revolutionary force, the new oppressor. No matter how free Marx portrays the utopian communist state of existence, it is impossible to achieve because of the sinner's alienation from self, others, and the world. Only by Jesus Christ submitting himself to the oppressive acts of humans against their Creator can there be, by humans living in faith-union with him, eternal release from the oppressive conditions that face fallen humanity (Isa. 53:7; Rom. 5:6–11).

Created in God's image, the human heart cries out for reconciliation of all contending factors, for an environment in which the obstructions to peaceful coexistence are removed and human suffering is finally over. Marx's earthly hope of peace and reconciliation is really hopelessness, and that hopelessness is the result

---

23. Jean-Paul Sartre, *Existentialism and Human Emotions*, trans. Bernard Frechtman (New York: Philosophical Library, 1985), 23.

of his version of hope. In contrast, God has acted in history with true hope; he has provided a living hope through the death and resurrection of his Son (1 Peter 1:3–5, 20–21). The hope for the Christian is assured by clinging by faith to what God the Father has done in his Son. By living out the biblical text, the Christian can see clearly why authentic, biblical "eschatology has become the large mountain of offense lying across the pathway of modern unbelief."[24] Indeed, Marx was repulsed by the eschatology of the Bible, and he exchanged it for a lie. His theory of history suppressed the ultimate truth: peace and reconciliation found only in the Prince of Peace, Jesus Christ.

24. Geerhardus Vos, *The Pauline Eschatology*, 4th printing (Grand Rapids: Eerdmans, 1972), vii. A serious engagement with the eschatology of Christ and the New Testament epistles is needed in the life of the church and the Christian in order to navigate through the political climate of the world. The following works could prove quite helpful, in addition to Vos's *The Pauline Eschatology*: Vos, "Eschatology of the New Testament," in *Redemptive History and Biblical Interpretation: The Shorter Writings of Geerhardus Vos*, ed. Richard B. Gaffin, Jr. (Phillipsburg, NJ: Presbyterian and Reformed, 1980), 25–58; Vos, "Paul's Eschatological Concept of the Spirit," in *Redemptive History and Biblical Interpretation*, ed. Gaffin, 91–125; Vos, *The Eschatology of the Old Testament*, ed. James T. Dennison, Jr. (Phillipsburg, NJ: Presbyterian and Reformed, 2001); Vos, *Reformed Dogmatics*, vol. 5, *Eschatology*, trans. and ed. Richard B. Gaffin, Jr. (Bellingham, WA: Lexham Press, 2016); Vos, "Heavenly-Mindedness," in *Grace and Glory* (Edinburgh: Banner of Truth Trust, 1994), 103–23; Herman Ridderbos, *When the Time Had Fully Come* (Grand Rapids: Eerdmans, 1957); Ridderbos, *The Coming of the Kingdom*, trans. H. de Jongste, ed. Raymond O. Zorn (Philadelphia: Presbyterian and Reformed, 1969); Ridderbos, *Paul: An Outline of His Theology*, trans. John R. De Witt (Grand Rapids: Eerdmans, 1975); Richard B. Gaffin, Jr., *Resurrection and Redemption: A Study in Paul's Soteriology*, 2nd ed. (Phillipsburg, NJ: Presbyterian and Reformed, 1987); Richard B. Gaffin, Jr., *By Faith, Not by Sight: Paul and the Order of Salvation*, 2nd ed. (Phillipsburg, NJ: Presbyterian and Reformed, 2013); William D. Dennison, *Paul's Two-Age Construction and Apologetics* (Eugene, OR: Wipf & Stock, 2000); Dennison, *In Defense of the Eschaton*.

5

CONCLUDING REMARKS

Observing that Christian theology explains the origin of evil by referring to the fall of man, Marx argues that Christian theology *assumes* such a position as historical fact, but cannot *explain* the position as historical fact.[1] He claims that, by contrast, his communist position proceeds "from an *actual* economic fact: the worker becomes all the poorer the more wealth he produces, the more his production increases in power and range."[2] In saying that, Marx is attempting to establish that the product of labor is the objectification of the laborer—that it is the alien object that places the laborer in bondage to the master and the product. Marx saw an analogy for his position in religion: "The more man puts into God, the less he retains in himself. The worker puts his life into the object; but now his life no longer belongs to him but to the object."[3]

Marx thus illustrates the apostle Paul's affirmation by

---

1. Karl Marx, *Economic and Philosophic Manuscripts of 1844*, in MECW, 3:271.
2. Ibid., 271–72.
3. Ibid., 272.

exchanging the truth of the historical revelation of God's providence for a lie (Rom. 1:25). In order to construct his own economic natural history, Marx manufactures his own view of human alienation and estrangement (the fall), so that humanity can be redeemed. We have already noted the internal tension in Marx's thought with respect the original state of humanity. On the one hand, the original state consisted of the free needs for survival in a natural environment, to which humanity will return in the final communist state of existence (the eschaton). On the other hand, Marx characterizes the original ontological state of existence as one of alienated labor. In any case, Marx holds that the laborer must be freed from alienated labor as history moves toward communism. It is in grappling with the possibility of such a vision that the truth of the historical revelation of Christian theism comes to light. While Marx claims that the biblical view of sin is an assumption without explanation, the Christian claims, on the basis of the history recorded in Scripture, that the biblical view of sin is *clearly explained* from within the confines of the communist movement itself. Let us highlight some of those observations in review.

First, Marx's own life reveals the struggles and antagonism that existed within the communist movement itself during the nineteenth century. Harmony among the leadership was virtually nonexistent as factions vied for power. Second, such power struggles continued into the twentieth century, with conflicts between Bolsheviks and Mensheviks and between the approaches of Lenin and Stalin. Perhaps no more obvious evidence for the Christian view of sin exists than the passion and quest of communists for power, and, once it is achieved, the desire never to relinquish it. These realities of the fallen human condition guarantee that the final communist state will remain a mythology in the minds of those who seek it. Third, Marx's *fallible* position and analysis of socioeconomic political history has so fallen apart that within the Marxian tradition itself it is affirmed that no one can claim to be a true Marxist anymore. Significant components of Marx's theory have already crumbled on the stage of history. One thing that has not been mentioned so far is the emergence of the welfare state within the democratic-capitalist political economy. Many scholars have observed that once the proletariat was paid an income by the government not to work, the incentive for revolution by the proletariat strongly decreased. The respected ethical imperative of human labor during the Enlightenment and the nineteenth century began to dissipate when governments offered benefits for nonlabor. A return to the original natural state of the absence of the objectification of labor under communism may not seem so attractive to workers after all. If the government will supply all that is needed for survival, Marx's eschatological communist state is doomed in real history.

For Marx, the end defines the beginning of history; his understanding of history is inherently eschatological. His natural and material dialectical construct of history dissolves into mythology as an attempt to replace the biblical view of history. In terms of biblical eschatology, it disintegrates as another failed human construct of the present evil age. Marx's position is merely a human creation of finite abstraction, set against the reality of biblical revelation and its fourfold state of man as summarized in the WCF. After all, the eschatological view of history as revealed in God's holy Word is immune to the folly of human constructs. The biblical account remains intact, unscathed by Marx's failure. Marx could not even escape the relativism that characterizes every construct that rises up against God in this present evil age. His viewpoint will always have rivals from within and from without that assure its collapse on the plain of history.

This breakdown is why Van Til's resolution to the problem of the one and the many is so brilliant. Since humanity's fall into sin, the secular mind has always tried to solve the problem of unity and diversity (the one and the many), or, to put it another way, the universal and the particular, with relative projections. These prognoses disintegrate before the Trinitarian God of the Bible (the unity of God within the diversity of the three persons). The infinite and eternal God of the Bible provides the resolution to the problem of the one and the many—after all, his ontological being is beyond any limited and restricted conception set forth by finite human thought. The problem's resolution is found in the eternal and infinite God who never passes away, as opposed to any epistemological, metaphysical, ontological, and ethical proposition that fights for prominence, but is here today and gone tomorrow. The final, glorious resolution of unity and diversity in a communist state of existence, even in the visionary application of John Lennon's imagination, is only a projection of romantic delusion. On the contrary, the biblical age to come never passes away, since it is established by the Word of the Lord. As in the days of Elijah, God will always confound the foolish gods of every age, including the Baal of Marx—the historic movement of dialectical materialism within the political economy of temporal existence. Against such folly, the Christian says, "As for me and my house, we will serve the living and true God of history" (cf. Josh. 24:15).

GLOSSARY[1]

*alienation. Alienation is the process whereby people become foreign to the world they are living in.

a priori. Prior to experience.

*bourgeoisie. The class of people in bourgeois society who own the social means of production as their private property, i.e., as capital.

*capitalism. The socioeconomic system where social relations are based on *commodities for exchange*, in particular private ownership of the means of production, and on the exploitation of wage-labor.

*class. A group of people sharing common relations to labor and the means of production.

*class struggle. Classes emerge at a certain stage in the development of the productive forces and the social division of labor, when there exists a social surplus of production,

1. https://www.marxists.org/encyclopedia/ (accessed May 24, 2016). Specifically Marxist terms are defined by this website. Definitions taken from this website are marked with an asterisk (*). Some terms do not appear here because they are defined in the text.

which makes it possible for one class to benefit by the expropriation of another. The conflict between classes there begins, founded in the division of the social surplus, and constitutes the fundamental antagonism in all classes.

*communism. To each according to his needs, from each according to his ability.

*dialectics. Dialectics is the method of reasoning which aims to understand things concretely in all their movement, change, and interconnection, with their opposite and contradictory sides in unity.

*distribution of labor. It is best to view this in the context of distribution, exchange, and the division of labor. Distribution and exchange only arise on the basis of a division of labor which creates a *separation* between production and consumption, and requires a socially determined means of mediating between the two.

*division of labor. The division of labor is a specific mode of cooperation wherein different tasks are assigned to different people. Division of labor is as old as labor itself, stretching back to the birth of the human race.

eschatology. Doctrine of the last things; the end time.

French structuralism. A movement popularized in France around the 1960s that maintained that there is an underlying system to human activity and language, by which human interaction and relationships can be analyzed.

German idealism. A movement in German philosophy from roughly 1770 to 1840 that held that reality consists of ideas and minds, of which the objects of experience are just appearances. Kant and Hegel are the most famous thinkers in this school.

guild system. In the feudal and modern eras, craftsmen in a particular craft (e.g., woodcarver, brick layer, blacksmith) had to apply for membership in the group, and, if received, had to agree to the methods and rules stated for the craft, receiving payment according to the level of skill they demonstrated.

immovable private property. Agrarian landed property.

*****materialism.** The philosophical trends that emphasize the material world (the world outside of consciousness) as the foundation and determinant of thinking, especially in relation to the question of the origin of knowledge.

*****means of production.** The tools (instruments) and the raw material (subject) used to create something (an object).

metaphysics. Study of the most real.

*****mode of production.** The method of producing the necessities of life (whether for health, food, housing, or needs such as education, science, nurturing, etc.).

movable private property. The capital that replaces landed property, which, by means of labor and exchange, damages social and economic equality.

*****private property.** Private property is the right of an individual to exclude others' use of an object, and predates the rupture of society into classes. In its undeveloped form, private property is the simple relation of the individual to the natural world in which one's individuality finds objective expression. Private property is essentially the denial of property to others and finds its ultimate expression in the relation of wage-labor and capital.

*****productive forces.** The productive forces are the unity of means of production and labor.

*****proletariat.** "The proletariat is that class in society which lives entirely from the sale of its labor power and does not draw profit from any kind of capital; whose weal and woe, whose life and death, whose sole existence depends on the demand for labor" (Fredrick Engels, *Principles of Communism*).

*****relations of production.** The objective material relations that exist in any society independently of human consciousness, formed between all people in the process of social production, exchange, and distribution of material wealth.

self-estrangement. Self-alienation.

sensuous world. The material world perceived by the senses.

*socialism. "The organization of society in such a manner that any individual, man or woman, finds at birth equal means for the development of their respective faculties and the utilization of their labor. The organization of society in such a manner that the exploitation by one person of the labor of his neighbor would be impossible, and where everyone will be allowed to enjoy the social wealth only to the extent of their contribution to the production of that wealth" (August Bebel, *Die Frau und der Sozialismus*).

species-being. The essential nature of humanity in consciousness, thought, and social interaction, in which the products of the capabilities of labor are the proof of life.

surplus-labor. When the worker extends his labor time, it provides no value to himself; it only provides surplus-value for the capitalist.

*surplus-value. Surplus-value is the social product that is over and above what is required for the producers to live.

BIBLIOGRAPHY

Primary

Marx, Karl, and Frederick Engels. *Collected Works*. 50 vols. New York: International Publishers, 1975–2004. Although the Marx-Engels-Gesamtausgabe (MEGA) project continues, of which over one hundred volumes are planned, the *Collected Works* (MECW) are the standard English translation of the initial volumes in that project.

Tucker, Robert C., ed. *The Marx-Engels Reader*. New York: W. W. Norton & Company, 1978. A fine introductory anthology of the writings of Marx and Engels for any beginning student.

Secondary

Acton, H. B. *The Illusion of the Epoch: Marxism-Leninism as a Philosophical Creed*. London: Cohen and West, 1955.

Althusser, Louis. *For Marx* (1965). Translated by Ben Brewster. London: Verso, 2005.

Bakhurst, David. "Marxism." In *Blackwell Companions to Philosophy:*

A Companion to Epistemology, edited by Jonathan Dancy and Ernest Sosa, 268–70. Oxford: Blackwell, 1992.

Bernstein, Eduard. "The Most Pressing Problems of Social Democracy" (1899). In *German Essays on Socialism in the Nineteenth Century,* edited by Frank Mecklenburg and Manfred Stassen, 120–38. New York: Continuum, 1990.

Bernstein, Richard J. *Praxis and Action.* Philadelphia: University of Pennsylvania Press, 1971. A significant work in understanding the important concept of praxis in social thought.

Carling, Alan, and Paul Wetherly. "Introduction: Rethinking Marx and History." *Science & Society* 70, 2 (April 2006): 146–54. Excellent introductory essay on the present state of affairs with respect to Marx's view of history.

Carver, Terrell. "Karl Marx." In *The Blackwell Guide to the Modern Philosophers: From Descartes to Nietzsche,* edited by Steven M. Emmanuel, 370–89. Malden: Blackwell Publishers, 2001. Carver is one of the most significant English-speaking scholars on Marx presently. His work on Marx, Marxism, and the Marxian tradition is informative and readable for students and scholars alike.

———. "The Manifesto in Marx's and Engels's Lifetimes." In *The Cambridge Companion to the Communist Manifesto,* edited by Terrell Carver and James Farr, 67–83. New York: Cambridge University Press, 2015.

———. *Marx and Engels: The Intellectual Relationship.* Bloomington: Indiana University Press, 1983.

———. "Marx and Marxism." In *The History of Continental Philosophy,* edited by Alan D. Schrift, vol. 2, *Nineteenth-Century Philosophy: Revolutionary Responses to the Existing Order,* edited by Alan D. Schrift and Daniel Conway, 35–63. Durham: Acumen, 2010.

———. "The Marxian Tradition." In *The Oxford Handbook of the History of Political Philosophy,* edited by George Klosko, 393–413. Oxford: Oxford University Press, 2011.

Chadwick, Owen. *The Secularization of the European Mind in the Nineteenth Century.* Cambridge: Cambridge University Press, 1975.

Cohen, G. A. *Karl Marx's Theory of History: A Defense*. Princeton: Princeton University Press, 1978. This volume is perhaps the most significant work on Marx's philosophy of history written in the last quarter of the twentieth century. It continues to occupy a central position in the discussion of the topic.

Dumont, Louis. *From Mandeville to Marx: The Genesis and Triumph of Economic Ideology*. Chicago: University of Chicago Press, 1977.

Elster, Jon. *An Introduction to Karl Marx*. Cambridge: Cambridge University Press, 1986.

―――. *Making Sense of Marx*. Cambridge: Cambridge University Press, 1986. Both volumes by Elster are helpful introductory discussions of Marx and the evolution of Marxist thought.

Gramsci, Antonio. *Selections from the Prison Notebooks of Antonio Gramsci*. Edited and translated by Quintin Hoare and Geoffrey Nowell Smith. New York: International Publishers, 2003.

Habermas, Jürgen. *Theory and Practice*. Translated by John Viertel. Boston: Beacon Press, 1974. A superb critical study of the attempt to synthesize theory and praxis in socio-political thought.

Hodgson, Peter C. *Shapes of Freedom: Hegel's Philosophy of World History in Theological Perspective*. Oxford: Oxford University Press, 2012.

Hook, Sidney. *From Hegel to Marx: Studies in the Intellectual Development of Karl Marx*. Ann Arbor: University of Michigan Press, 1962.

―――. *Marx and the Marxists*. Princeton: D. Van Nostrand, 1955. Any study of Marx by Hook is worth reading; his work on the Young Hegelians and Marx's relationship to them is a must read.

Iggers, Georg G. *New Directions in European Historiography*. Middletown, CT: Wesleyan University Press, 1975.

Johnson, Paul. *Intellectuals*. New York: Harper Perennial, 1988.

Kolakowski, Leszek. *Main Currents of Marxism: I. The Founders*. Translated by P. S. Falla. Oxford: Oxford University Press, 1978. Highly respected study on the history of Marxism, especially its principal players.

Levine, Norman. *Marx's Discourse with Hegel*. Basingstoke: Palgrave Macmillan, 2012.

Lowith, Karl. *Meaning in History*. Chicago: University of Chicago Press, 1949.

Lukács, Georg. *History of Class Consciousness: Studies in Marxist Dialectics* (1922). Translated by Rodney Livingstone. Cambridge, MA: MIT Press, 1983. Crucial study of the dialectical method of Marx and the Marxists as it is mapped out in history between the classes of society.

McLellan, David. *Karl Marx: His Life and Thought*. New York: Harper & Row, 1973.

McLennan, Gregor. *Marxism and the Methodologies of History*. London: Verso, 1981. A fine biography of Marx that should be consulted by those who want to understand the context of his thought in synthesis with his life journey.

Peffer, R. G. *Marxism, Morality, and Social Justice*. Princeton: Princeton University Press, 1990.

Rader, Melvin. *Marx's Interpretation of History*. New York: Oxford University Press, 1979. Important study in the context of the emergence of Cohen's work on Marx's philosophy of history.

Sartre, Jean-Paul. *Existentialism and Human Emotions*. Translated by Bernard Frechtman. New York: Philosophical Library, 1985.

———. *The Ghost of Stalin* (1956). Translated by Martha H. Fletcher with the assistance of John R. Kleinschmidt. New York: George Braziller, 1967.

———. *Search for a Method*. Translated with an introduction by Hazel E. Barnes. New York: Vintage Books, 1968.

Shaw, William M. *Marx's Theory of History*. Stanford: Stanford University Press, 1978. Important study in the context of the emergence of Cohen's work on Marx's philosophy of history.

Sperber, Jonathan. *Karl Marx: A Nineteenth-Century Life*. New York: Liveright Publishing, 2013. A fine biography of Marx that places his life in the context of his own times.

Tucker, Robert. *Philosophy and Myth in Karl Marx*. 2nd ed. Cambridge: Cambridge University Press, 1972. Anything written by Tucker on Marx and Engels is worth reading. This volume is an excellent engagement with Marx's thought. It will challenge any student of Marx.

———. *Stalin as a Revolutionary, 1879–1929: A Study in History and Personality*. New York: W. W. Norton & Company, 1973.

Van Til, Cornelius. *The Doctrine of Scripture*. Phillipsburg, NJ: Presbyterian and Reformed, 1967.

Vos, Geerhardus. *The Pauline Eschatology*. 4th printing. Grand Rapids: Eerdmans, 1972.

Recommended for Further Reading

Biography

McLellan, David. *Karl Marx: His Life and Thought*. New York: Harper & Row, 1973. A fine biography of Marx that should be consulted by those who want to understand the context of his thought in synthesis with his life journey.

Sperber, Jonathan. *Karl Marx: A Nineteenth-Century Life*. New York: Liveright Publishing, 2013. A fine biography of Marx that places his life in the context of his own times. Well written and easy to read.

Primary

Tucker, Robert C., ed. *The Marx-Engels Reader*. New York: W. W. Norton & Company, 1978. Tucker provides a fine introductory anthology of the writings of Marx and Engels. His selections and abridged readings for the beginning student of the Marx-Engels corpus are excellent.

Secondary

Carling, Alan, and Paul Wetherly. "Introduction: Rethinking Marx and History." *Science & Society* 70, 2 (April 2006): 146–54. Excellent introductory essay on the present state of affairs with respect to Marx's view of history.

Carver, Terrell. "Marx and Marxism." In *The History of Continental*

Philosophy, edited by Alan D. Schrift, vol. 2, *Nineteenth-Century Philosophy: Revolutionary Responses to the Existing Order*, edited by Alan D. Schrift and Daniel Conway, 35–63. Durham: Acumen, 2010.

———. "The Marxian Tradition." In *The Oxford Handbook of the History of Political Philosophy*, edited by George Klosko, 393–413. Oxford: Oxford University Press, 2011. Carver is currently one of the most important English-speaking scholars of Marx. These two articles provide a helpful introduction to Marx, Marxism, and the Marxian tradition.

Cohen, G. A. *Karl Marx's Theory of History: A Defense*. Princeton: Princeton University Press, 1978. This volume is perhaps the most important work on Marx's philosophy of history written in the last quarter of the twentieth century. It continues to occupy a central position in the discussion of the topic.

Elster, Jon. *An Introduction to Karl Marx*. Cambridge: Cambridge University Press, 1986.

———. *Making Sense of Marx*. Cambridge: Cambridge University Press, 1986. Both volumes by Elster are helpful introductory discussions of Marx and the evolution of Marxist thought.

Hook, Sidney. *From Hegel to Marx: Studies in the Intellectual Development of Karl Marx*. Ann Arbor: University of Michigan, 1962. Any study of Marx by Hook is worth reading; this work provides great insight into Marx's relationship with the Young Hegelians—a must read.

Rader, Melvin. *Marx's Interpretation of History*. New York: Oxford University Press, 1979. Both Rader and Shaw (below) introduce the student to the immediate discussion and debate regarding Cohen's work on Marx's philosophy of history.

Shaw, William M. *Marx's Theory of History*. Stanford: Stanford University Press, 1978.

Tucker, Robert. *Philosophy and Myth in Karl Marx*. 2nd ed. Cambridge: Cambridge University Press, 1972. Anything written by Tucker on Marx and Engels is challenging. This volume is an excellent engagement with Marx's thought. It will test any student of Marx.

INDEX OF SCRIPTURE

INDEX OF SUBJECTS AND NAMES

William D. Dennison (MDiv, ThM, Westminster Theological Seminary; PhD, Michigan State University) is professor of interdisciplinary studies at Covenant College and a fellow in apologetics at Greystone Theological Institute. He is a charter member of the Society of Christian Philosophers and the International Society of Christian Apologetics, as well as a member of the Evangelical Theological Society and the Association for Integrative Studies. His research interests include nineteenth- and twentieth-century German theology, philosophy, and history, especially the theology of Rudolf Bultmann. Dr. Dennison's publications include the highly acclaimed *The Young Bultmann: Context for His Understanding of God, 1884–1925* (New York: Peter Lang, 2008).

1. Confusion surrounding Marx?
   often seen as "founder of socialism", socialism = means
   to an end (utopian society), not the end goal

2. Beginning of Marxism tradition?
   publication of Communist manifesto, especially in pamphlet form,
   method of dialectic materialism,

3. Departure from orthodox Marxism?

4. Impact of Mega?